With deep appreciation, this book is dedicated to all the inquiring creative educators who have been an inspiration to me and a fountain of empowerment for their students.

Acknowledgments

Three things were required to write this book: a perspective on school improvement, an understanding of classroom and school experience, and support. I can truthfully assert that every teacher and mentor I've worked with contributed to the development of my perspective and my understanding of the collaborative inquiry process. I am sincerely thankful to all of them. However, the contributions of a few individuals and groups deserve special recognition.

Specifically, I want to thank Peter Senge and his associates for their work in helping all of us to understand the effectiveness and processes of the learning organization. The writing and work of Shirley Hord, Rick DuFour, Rebecca DuFour, and Robert Eaker have been invaluable in helping me and my colleagues in education to understand the importance of remaking our schools as professional learning communities. Their work has laid a foundation upon which we can expand the power of teamwork and collegiality in the service of high expectations for all of our students.

I want to give special thanks to the many teacher teams I have worked with and observed in the past few years. Their work has provided me with unbounded optimism about the future of teaching, as well as countless examples of how to conduct collaborative inquiries. By unselfishly sharing how they uncovered the information needed to improve their students' education, these educators have helped me understand the dynamics of teaching and learning and the power of the inquiry process more deeply than I ever could have without their assistance. I want to specifically acknowledge all that I learned from the teacher teams of the Great Expectations Program in Kansas City (Missouri), the Goal III Teachers of the Killeen Unified School District (Texas), the Title 1 Teams from the Washoe County School District (Nevada), as well as all the school and district teams that came together over the years to create Project LEARN (League of Educational Action Researchers in the Northwest). It was by observing your creativity and initiative that I became a true believer in the power of inquiry for transforming schools.

Yet, even with the good foundation provided by these scholars, educators, and practitioners, it would have been impossible for me to have crafted a worthwhile text were it not for the patience, tolerance, and assistance of Robb Clouse, the publisher at Solution Tree Press. He assembled a group of thoughtful reviewers who gently (and occasionally, not so gently) pointed out where this manuscript was in need of revision. This book simply could not have been completed without the critical insights and suggestions of these reviewers and the expert help of senior editor Edward Levy.

Lastly, I want to express my deepest thanks and affection for Annette Skaugset of the graduate school at Lewis & Clark College, who not only gave up her weekends to assist in typing, editing, and retyping the text, but did so cheerfully. I know I would never have completed this manuscript without the positive encouragement and support I received from Annette.

While there is only one author whose name appears on this book, I would have had nothing to write were it not for what I've learned from all the wonderful educators I've been privileged to work with. Ultimately, my understanding of the power of action research for school improvement is testimony to the personal growth that comes from professional collaboration and team learning. From the bottom of my heart, I thank you all.

—Richard Sagor
Camas, Washington, December 2009

* * *

Solution Tree Press would like to thank the following reviewers:

Diane Benavides
Instructional Coordinator
Neff Elementary
Houston, Texas

Emily F. Calhoun
Director, Phoenix Alliance
St. Simons Island, Georgia

Jan Lyons
Principal
Sylmar High School
Sylmar, California

Virginia Mahlke
Retired Elementary School Principal
Fairfax County Public Schools
Fairfax, Virginia

Avery R. Mitchell
Principal
Albemarle Road Middle School
Charlotte, North Carolina

Jan Morrison
Project Director
Washoe County School District
Reno, Nevada

Tamara Holmlund Nelson
Assistant Professor
Department of Teaching and Learning
Washington State University Vancouver
Vancouver, Washington

Mary Ann Van Doornik
Ninth Grade Language Arts Teacher
Marcus Whitman Junior High
Port Orchard, Washington

Elsa Wright
Assistant Principal
Aldine Ninth Grade School
Aldine, Texas

Diane Yendol-Hoppey
Professor and Benedum Collaborative Director
West Virginia University
Morgantown, West Virginia

Table of Contents

Titles in italic indicate reproducible pages.

Visit **go.solution-tree.com/plcbooks** to download the reproducibles in this book.

Habit of Inquiry 2

Articulating Theories of Action 29

Habit of Inquiry 3

Acting Purposefully While Collecting Data 53

Epilogue

Appendix

About the Author

Richard Sagor is the founding director of the Institute for the Study of Inquiry in Education (ISIE), a consulting service dedicated to advancing the capacity of local school faculties.

Educated in the public schools of New York, Dick received his BA from New York University before moving to the Pacific Northwest, where he earned two MA degrees and a PhD in curriculum and instruction from the University of Oregon.

Before entering higher education, Dick had fourteen years of public school administrative experience, including service as an assistant superintendent, high school principal, instruction vice principal, disciplinary vice principal, and alternative school head teacher. He has taught a range of students, from the gifted to the learning challenged, in the areas of social studies, reading, and written composition.

In the spring of 2008, Dick retired from his position as professor and director of the Educational Leadership Program at Lewis & Clark College in Portland, Oregon. Prior to Lewis & Clark, he served as a professor of educational leadership at Washington State University and directed Project LEARN (the League of Educational Action Researchers in the Northwest).

Dick has extensive consulting experience. He has worked as a site visitor for the United States Department of Education's Blue Ribbon Schools Program and has consulted with numerous state departments of education and hundreds of independent school districts across North America. He has also provided staff development workshops for international schools in Asia, South America, and Africa. His consulting is focused primarily on data and standards-based school improvement, professional learning communities, collaborative action research, teacher motivation, leadership development, and teaching at-risk youth.

His articles on school reform and action research have received awards from the National Association of Secondary School Principals and the Educational Press Association of America. Dick has written nine books, including *Guiding School Improvement with Action Research*, *The Action Research Guidebook: A Four-Step Stage Process for Educators and School Teams*, *Motivating Students and Teachers in an Era of Standards*, *At-Risk Students: Reaching and Teaching Them*, and *The TQE Principal: A Transformed Leader.*

Preface

This book was designed to assist individual teachers, groups of teachers, and school leaders who work with professional learning community (PLC) teams to become disciplined and deliberative with data as they design and implement program improvements to enhance student learning. The evidence suggests that when this occurs, not only do students prosper, but the school culture becomes enriched and teachers enjoy greater professional satisfaction (WestEd, 2000; Garmston, 2005).

It is the premise of this book that collaborative inquiry is the sine qua non of a PLC. Without constant and high-quality collaborative inquiry, a PLC simply can't be sustained.

A culture of collaborative inquiry emerges once a specific mindset takes hold in the school—a mindset grown from five particular habits of inquiry: (1) clarifying a shared vision for success; (2) articulating theories of action; (3) acting purposefully while collecting data; (4) analyzing data collaboratively; and (5) using informed team action planning.

Many readers will recognize the practices represented by these five habits as the *action research process*. The phrase *action research* was first coined by Kurt Lewin (1951), and the practices that make up this process have been discussed in dozens of books since then. In my own work with collaborative teacher learning teams, I have referred to the team inquiry process as *collaborative action research* (Sagor, 1992a, 2000, 2005). However, even in places where no one has heard this term, this mindset and the five habits of inquiry have become integral to the conduct of professional work. Wherever this has occurred, schools have been transformed into powerful professional learning communities, even if they didn't label themselves as such.

Following an introductory chapter exploring the concept of professional learning, we will examine each of the five essential habits of inquiry needed to make collaborative inquiry a routine professional behavior in a school.

Equity and Excellence

Even many high-performing schools still invest heavily in the work of their PLC teams. One might ask, Why would schools in which most students are already performing well above average be concerned about professional learning? The reason is that good is rarely good enough for a professional. As long as a single student or category of students isn't realizing his or her potential, professional teachers feel their work isn't done. We join together as a PLC primarily to determine how to help every one of our students perform excellently. While it is assumed that readers of this book will be conducting action research on a variety of topics, it is also assumed that each inquiry will focus on the same fundamental question: "What will it take for us to achieve universal student success?" I have taken this stance because I believe that with enough collaboration, creativity, and focused effort, professional educators can close any and all achievement gaps.

The Action Research Process

This book is primarily designed to help the faculty of a school or district become engaged in the collaborative action research process, but it is also designed as a guide for school leadership. That is why, throughout the book, the reader will find Leadership Notes, boxed suggestions, for leaders of schools who wish to see themselves functioning as PLCs. If you are a principal, superintendent, or teacher leader with responsibility for helping your school become a PLC, you may want to refer to these leadership notes for suggestions on how to foster faculty morale while supporting staff success with the five essential habits of inquiry.

I have often thought that the culture of PLCs is analogous to a set of Russian nesting dolls. Each subculture rests inside a series of larger ones. Likewise, the individual teacher, who is herself a professional learner, works inside a grade-level or disciplinary team that operates inside a larger professional learning community. The assumption is that these PLC teams in turn reside inside school faculties that, being committed to continuous improvement, have defined themselves as a professional learning community. Hopefully, in many cases the school itself is nested inside a district that shares this perspective and is committed to promoting and supporting professional learning.

Because members of each PLC team are also participants in their school's and district's PLCs, it is hoped that the learning that occurs within each team will have an impact on the members of the larger professional learning community of which they are a part.

Throughout you will find hypothetical teacher and classroom examples based on my personal experience and that of classroom teachers implementing this process. It is perfectly appropriate to adjust these strategies to fit your situation or to substitute alternative approaches of your own design. At its heart, action research is a creative rather than prescriptive process.

It is my hope that reflecting on the ideas and exploring the exercises outlined in this guide will enhance your love of teaching and enable you to find increased joy in your students' learning. May your work as an action researcher unleash your creativity and breathe life into the concepts of *professional learning*, *community of learners*, and *professionalism* in your school.

Introduction
Being a Professional
Means Being a Learner

The word *professional* has a nice ring to it, but though we use it frequently, we seldom pause to reflect on its meaning. It is a normal adult routine to search for and secure a job, but becoming a professional requires years of preparation and planning. Furthermore, the choice of a profession usually indicates a person's commitment to investing the better part of one's lifetime in a single pursuit.

What makes someone a professional? In athletics, it's simply being paid for your work. But that minimalist definition obscures an essential truth: even with hard work, passion, and commitment, not everyone can become a professional athlete. Simply offering yourself for employment doesn't gain you a position on a major league team. That opportunity is extended only to those who have demonstrated a profound mastery of their craft.

Qualities That Define Professionals

Fundamentally, all professionals are expected to bring two qualities to their work:

1. Mastery of their field's knowledge base

2. The ability to craft creative solutions to nonroutine problems

Mastery of Their Field's Knowledge Base

Successful professionals need to be on top of (or at least capable of accessing) all that is known by practitioners in their field. We expect lawyers to know the law, doctors to know medicine, and architects to know architecture. In education, we are expected to develop content mastery through our preservice training, by staying current with professional reading, and by attending in-service programs. Hopefully, through these activities, we end up with a working knowledge of the profession's knowledge. Schools, universities, and collaborative faculty study teams can play a critical role in helping us stay current with developments in the domains of learning, curriculum, and instruction. But as essential as mastery of the knowledge base is, it is not sufficient to qualify us as professionals.

The best way to appreciate the inadequacy of knowledge alone is to ask yourself this question: "Would I trust someone with my most perplexing problems simply because he or she might possess expert knowledge?" I expect you would answer with an emphatic, "No!"

I'll illustrate with a hypothetical example. I used to teach at the high school level, and I am confident that I could effectively facilitate a class on pediatrics to a group of typical high school students. Furthermore, I am pretty certain that in one semester, by employing mastery learning techniques, I could have every one of my students fully capable of diagnosing and prescribing the appropriate treatment for the fifty most common childhood illnesses. For the purpose of this illustration, put away your concerns for a moment about legal and licensing issues. Simply imagine these students diligently working in an after-school clinic where their expertise is offered to neighborhood families. For a fraction of the cost of going to an expensive pediatric practice, local families can visit our clinic, get an accurate diagnosis, and receive appropriate direction on how to treat their child's condition. If you accept the premise behind my hypothetical, that high school students can be trained in pediatrics, why do we persist in taking our children to clinics staffed by professional medical personnel?

There is, of course, one very good reason. I am confident that my high school students could provide adequate pediatric care—if all children were identical. However, we know all children are not identical. What if your child's response to a particular ear infection isn't what the pediatric textbook predicted? What if her response to amoxicillin didn't match the pharmaceutical literature? What would my well-trained teenage diagnosticians do in such a circumstance? In reality, it is unlikely they would know how to respond when a patient behaves atypically. This brings us to the second critical element of professional practice: the ability to craft creative solutions to nonroutine problems.

Ability to Craft Creative Solutions to Nonroutine Problems

I am someone who enjoys do-it-yourself endeavors. People like me look for things we can do for ourselves. When a drain is clogged, I use a plunger before calling the plumber. When I buy a car, I don't feel a need to consult a lawyer, and when planning a family dinner, I don't phone a nutritionist.

Basically, when the issue I am grappling with is routine, implementing a proven practice with fidelity is the most efficient way to proceed. However, when the water pressure falls precipitously, if the sales contract I'm being asked to sign is complex and filled with ambiguous language, or I have a family member who suffers from food allergies, I am reluctant to go it alone. These are all situations that are unlikely to be solved with textbook remedies; solving them will require the insights and creativity of a skilled professional.

When I call a professional, I don't demand a quick and simple answer. After all, if the answer were obvious, I'd already have figured it out. What I need is the assistance of someone who, based on knowledge and experience, will be able to ask the right questions and creatively craft a solution appropriate to my situation.

This kind of wisdom, honed through a disciplined and deliberate analysis of data from experience solving nonroutine problems, can't easily be conveyed through an in-service training program. By necessity, training programs focus on the usual, the routine. For educators, the best source of wisdom regarding the solution of nonroutine problems comes from insights developed through your own action research and refined through meaningful collaborative work and discourse with colleagues.

Collaborative action research and PLC teamwork can provide a teacher with a type of professional learning that is unavailable anywhere else.

The Art and Science of Teaching

For millennia, it has been debated whether teaching is more science than art or more art than science. Great educators seem to be both artists and scientists. They are artists at making learning come alive for a variety of students, but equally important, they employ practices, draw upon principles, and master techniques that maximize the effectiveness of their instructional artistry.

School systems have tended to rely on the use of outside designers to develop their interventions. Frequently, the designers of curriculum and the authors of district-adopted instructional programs are unfamiliar with the unique attributes of the students working in a particular school context. Unfortunately, the classical division of labor in education has separated those who design educational innovations from those who carry them out.

The collaborative action research process remedies this situation. It merges the art and science of teaching by recognizing the critical role of teacher as designer. It empowers local educators to design techniques and strategies that promise to help all students achieve mastery of priority school objectives. The teacher who simultaneously teaches his or her classes while discerning the answers to the most perplexing problems of educational design is the truly complete professional educator—someone who is employing the best of the field's knowledge base while creating novel solutions for nonroutine problems.

Another profession where both art and science are intertwined is architecture. The architect must bring to his or her work extensive knowledge from a number of fields. The architect must have extensive knowledge of the laws of physics, civil engineering, and material science. But to create a finished product that both addresses the expectations of the client and can be constructed in a unique setting requires both artistry and creativity.

In this book we will often refer to teachers as educational architects. Like architects, teachers must have a solid background—in this case, in the science of teaching and learning. They must also be able to design curriculum, instruction, and assessments, and organize and creatively deliver all three to achieve the maximum benefit for each of their unique students. And, as in architecture, just as there will never be a single house plan that is aesthetically pleasing to everyone, suitable for every family, and adaptable to every site, there will never be a single formula for successfully teaching every unique child in every classroom. The metaphor of teacher as educational architect incorporates the understanding that there are often multiple designs (teaching strategies) that are equally capable of producing wonderful results with students. The collaborative action research process will help you creatively design educational plans that fit the needs of your diverse learners.

Fidelity of Implementation

It is often argued that the route to quality education is through mandating the adoption of proven practices (McIntyre et al., 2005; Wallace, Blasé, Fixsen, & Naoom, 2008). This approach has some obvious appeal. Upon reflection, however, it becomes clear that it is premised on the flawed assumption that one size could fit all teachers and simultaneously meet the needs of all students. I have called this the *one-solution syndrome* (Sagor, 1995). Policies that mandate a single intervention are built from a perspective that everything and every student are "routine." As with my imaginary pediatrics clinic staffed by high school students, the "nonroutine child" simply isn't taken into consideration. This worldview never made much sense, but is more problematic now than ever. The fact is, student diversity in American classrooms is the greatest it has ever been, and is steadily increasing.

Moreover, for all the attention given to proven practices, I have yet to hear of any single meaningful instructional strategy that has been shown to produce universal student success. Cardiologists accept the fact that no single medicine or procedure will cure all heart disease, yet they continue to treat every patient who comes to them. They don't reject patients who don't respond to a particular protocol. They work with them by adapting established and novel treatments to best meet their needs. The same must become true for educators. A professional orientation in schools doesn't mean having a ready-made solution for every problem. Rather, it means recognizing that helping every student achieve maximum success requires adapting, adjusting, and redesigning the educational process until that student does, in fact, succeed.

Intuitively, professional teachers know that whatever the data regarding an adopted proven practice, that practice could not have possibly succeeded with *every one of* the students they face daily in class. They know that an expectation that they robotically implement a program with fidelity will inevitably lead to certain students being left behind. Unfortunately, such expectations are too common in today's schools. For example, the following statements were published on the website of the Los Angeles Unified School District (LAUSD, n.d.):

> Fidelity of implementation occurs when teachers use the instructional strategies and deliver the content of the curricula in the same way that they were designed to be used and delivered.

> Critical to the fidelity of the implementation of a curriculum is the importance of teaching the lessons in the order that the publisher has presented them. Teachers are also to teach each lesson according to the publisher's recommended time. Furthermore, teachers are instructed to follow the recommendation of the publisher about how many lessons to teach per week. In addition, teachers are to

make use of each publisher's recommended questions and homework pages or activity sheets that will give students the opportunity to practice the skill they are learning. In brief, all of the publishers have specific recommendations for their programs that teachers should follow.

When the expectation is for "fidelity of implementation" and teachers are told to withhold their creativity and avoid deviations from the adopted instructional protocol, what is likely to happen to the nonroutine student? For the routine student, the one for whom the proven practice was designed, implementation with fidelity may be exactly what is needed. But it is not uncommon to find that even the finest scientifically based proven practices aren't effective with high percentages of students (Allington, 2002). Like a sick patient who is repeatedly given a treatment that isn't working, the nonroutine student who is forced to endure instruction that doesn't fit will fail to improve.

Professional Problem Solving

Professionals approach problems by asking what the client wishes to accomplish, what has been getting in the way of the client's success, what might explain the difficulties the client has been encountering, and based on the evidence and the wisdom gleaned from experience, what could be done differently? In schools that have become professional learning communities, these questions are confronted regularly by each PLC team. Adequately answering them calls for collaborative action research conducted by individual teachers and collaborative teams who skillfully develop and exercise the following five specific habits of inquiry.

Habit 1: Clarifying a Shared Vision for Success

Lewis Carroll wrote, "If you don't know where you are going, any road will get you there." The first habit of inquiry required of all educational architects is to hold a clear view of a future reality in which all students evidence success with program goals. This habit isn't demonstrated by being able to enunciate boilerplate objectives using the current educational lingo. True mastery of this habit requires the ability to describe student success to students, parents, and colleagues in terms that are both clear and unambiguous.

Habit 2: Articulating Theories of Action

Even those who know where they are going are not necessarily on the best road to get there. There are often multiple routes to a single destination. This second habit of mind is developed by internalizing a set of processes that help us reason our way through the selection of routes to our desired goals. A "theory of action" is simply a well-thought-through route to a goal, built from both the profession's knowledge base and the wisdom of our own practice, with real potential for producing universal student success. Fundamentally, whenever student success occurs, it has resulted from a series of things that went right. Educational architects who have demonstrated mastery of this habit are able to clearly justify the rationale behind each of their instructional decisions.

Habit 3: Acting Purposefully While Collecting Data

Often, in professional work, the decision to employ a particular intervention or action is an experiment. Determining the actual effectiveness of these experiments is critical if we are to learn from our experience. Therefore, it is important to collect relevant data on the adequacy of the theories of action we are following. One has shown mastery of Habit 3 once it has become routine to stop before acting and ask, "What is it I will need to know about my teaching, and what data should I be collecting to help me answer my questions?"

Habit 4: Analyzing Data Collaboratively

Today's teachers are swimming in data. Most have a pretty good idea how their students are performing. The more difficult questions teachers face are why a particular student is where he or she is, what factors enabled this student to acquire the skill, and what inhibited his or her success. By mastering the habit of data analysis, both teachers and students are able to learn from their past successes and missteps.

Habit 5: Using Informed Team Action Planning

PLC teams are powerful entities. When they are functioning well, their very existence provides evidence that several minds are better than one. However, just because something is a group activity doesn't make it superior to an individual pursuit. This habit of inquiry requires internalizing the skills of collaborative analysis, thereby ensuring that the end result of group exploration is truly superior to what any member might have produced by relying on his or her own devices. Mastering this habit requires developing a perspective on student learning as a shared responsibility.

Caveats, Assumptions, and Suggestions

In the chapters that follow, we will work through the collaborative action research process. The reader will receive step-by-step directions on the use of tactics and strategies that others have used with each step. By following these steps and implementing the suggested strategies or designing your own customized alternatives, you will reinforce the five habits of inquiry while becoming a more creative and effective educational architect. Before proceeding, I want to alert you to several assumptions regarding the critical educational issues that inform this text and some suggestions and caveats to keep in mind as you proceed through the action research process.

Equity

Throughout this book it will be taken as a given that our goal as educators is *universal student success*. When discussing an achievement target that a team might be pursuing, it will be assumed that the goal is to see every single student demonstrate proficiency on that target. I am not so naive as to believe that any one person or team using this process for the first time will accomplish this goal. It is also unlikely to be achieved even after several cycles of collaborative action research. It is, however, important to be clear that this is our goal. Frequently, we will hear of goals that declare an expectation that 80 or 90 percent of the students will become successful. Writing goals this way implies that it is expected and considered acceptable for some students to miss the mark. As professional educators and members of a PLC team, our goal should be to learn whatever it takes to enable us to create the conditions in which every child will succeed.

Time

The greatest frustration of classroom teachers everywhere is the four-letter word *time*. Be assured that I understand and appreciate that few readers have lots of available time on their hands to devote to new pursuits.

While internalizing these five habits of inquiry and conducting action research does take time, it need not be an onerous experience. All time demands aren't created equal. Time investments that help us do our work better are ones we gladly make. Consider the football coaching staff at virtually every high school: basically, a high school football staff is a PLC team that conducts collaborative action research each week of the season. They hold a shared vision of success (winning), develop theories of action designed to realize their vision (their practice plans), engage in formative assessment (the game), pour over data on student performance (game films), reflect on the results, and as a consequence, modify their teaching (the practice plan for the following week). Since the collaborative action research cycle helps the coaches become more successful, they happily invest the time necessary to make the process work.

On the other hand, educators are right to resist time demands that have little payback in terms of student performance. This goes to the heart of the functioning of a PLC team. In schools where PLC teams function effectively and time spent with the team is valued by its members, inevitably, the team is engaged in collaborative action research (even when it's not called by that name). In such teams, time spent figuring out what works and how it worked with real students is understood to pay dividends. We also have significant evidence that teachers find that time spent conducting action research on priority objectives adds richness to their professional lives, rather than detracting from them (Sagor, 1992b, 1995).

Correlation

I am someone who likes to have definitive answers to my questions. This is as true with my teaching as it is with my personal life. I want to know precisely what causes a student to succeed, and I long for the certainty that comes from finding a clean set of cause-and-effect relationships. Alas, that will never be the case. In the world of social science, outside of a controlled laboratory, it is impossible to establish causation. There are simply too many variables that influence human decisions and actions. Even identical twins won't always respond the same way to the same stimuli. This means that your action research won't allow you to prove with finality that X causes Y. That being said, you will still be able to establish what works. This is done by identifying powerful correlations. When you can say to yourself and others with confidence,

"When I do this, this happens," you will have established a powerful correlation. While you may not have established causality in a scientific or philosophical sense, you will have uncovered strategies that are well worth repeating.

Sample Size

One question often asked by people new to action research is, "From how many students do I need to collect data to make my research valid and reliable?" The answer is, "It depends." I

Definitions

There are several key terms and phrases that you will encounter as you work your way through this book. Some may be new to you, and some are defined differently in different contexts. The following definitions are provided to clarify what these terms mean in the context of the collaborative action research process.

achievement target. A measurable component of a goal. Goals are realized once students have mastered each component achievement target.

community. A group of individuals bound together by a shared interest

goal. A measurable outcome that constitutes a significant aspect of an overall school or program vision

learning. The process of discovering something new or gaining enhanced insights into a phenomena of interest

personal vision. A robust picture of a reality in which one's hopes and dreams have been realized

PLC team. A defined group, officially sanctioned or expected to work together for the purpose of addressing the challenges of teaching and learning

professional. Any educated practitioner, working in a field possessing a dynamic knowledge base, who is routinely asked to craft creative solutions for nonroutine client problems

professional learning community. Any organization in which it has become the norm for the professionals to collaborate with others for the express purpose of enhancing understanding and improving student learning. Membership in a professional learning community implies routine engagement in professional learning with others who share common interests.

shared vision. A robust description of a reality where the hopes and dreams of the professional learning community have been realized

theory of action. A well-thought-through plan based on the professional knowledge base and the wisdom of practice, with potential for producing universal student success

universal student success. Achievement of proficiency on a standard by each and every student, regardless of prior history or demographic characteristics

recall one team that routinely collected data from a student body of 1,400 students. But I have also seen excellent studies conducted with data collected from a single student. How large a sample size you employ should be determined by the phenomena you are seeking to understand and the amount of time you have available.

As a general rule, the smaller the sample size, the deeper you can go with your investigation. So, for example, if you were interested in understanding the general attitudes of the students toward the curriculum, a broad statistical review of enrollment trends and a survey of all affected students would be a productive way to assemble your data. However, if you wanted to know how well students understood the specific scientific principles you taught in class, a review of the collective experience of one class of thirty students might suffice. And if your interest was in understanding the cognitive development process involved in the acquisition of a particular math concept, an investigation into the experience and learning of a few selected students might be ideal.

Number of Strategies to Include

Some readers of this book may approach it with a specific action research project in mind. Others may decide to make use of every single strategy offered here exactly as presented. If you do, I trust you will enjoy the work, and I believe it will help you discover the answers to your questions. But unless you have the assistance of a functioning and supportive PLC team, you may find using all of these techniques and strategies cumbersome and overly time consuming. For this reason, I encourage you to use this book as a guide or an outline. Read each chapter from beginning to end as you approach that aspect of the action research process. After reading each habit of inquiry and becoming familiar with that part of the collaborative action research process, it will be up to you to pick and choose the strategies that you feel best fit your project. Feel free to modify any procedure or technique if you feel that will make it a better fit for your particular inquiry. A roadmap of the essential elements of the five-stage action research process can be found on page 140.

It is also fine to abbreviate the process; some excellent action research projects have been completed with data obtained in a single school day. While it isn't essential that you follow every procedure as outlined, it is important that every inquiry minimally involve the use of each of the five essential habits of inquiry. Furthermore, it is critical that you work your way through the first three habits and complete a data collection plan prior to initiating a study.

I expect some teams will spend the better part of a school year on a single project. In such cases, the team members may be well served by following each strategy exactly as presented. Proceeding this way will provide an excellent opportunity to practice each of the five habits. There will likely be other cases where readers or teams will want to get answers to their questions in one month's time or less. Be assured this can be accomplished while still keeping faith with the action research process, providing that conscious attention is given to each of the five habits of inquiry.

Habit of Inquiry
Clarifying a Shared Vision for Success

1

This chapter introduces the first habit of inquiry needed by those engaged in the practice of educational architecture: a clear shared vision to guide their work when they are planning for teaching and learning. This chapter—and this entire book—are built on one assumption: the overarching justification for our work as professional educators and the rationale for investing our time with a PLC team are the pursuit of universal student success. This is extremely difficult and challenging work. What makes it so challenging is that we are trying to accomplish something that has eluded and confounded us up until now.

In areas where we are happy with our past success, it is usually a mistake, as well as a waste of our energy and the time of our colleagues, to spend our limited collaborative planning time documenting our successful practices in great detail. While it might be helpful for an external university researcher, spending PLC team time producing such documentation will provide little added benefit for our current students.

In terms of collaborative planning, the wise thing to do in areas where we've been successful is to take note of what worked and stay the course. However, in areas where we are unhappy with past results, it is imperative for us to try something new. If we are dissatisfied with the performance of our students yet continue to conduct business as we have in the past, there is no logical justification for expecting different results. This book is devoted to the exploration of a straightforward and disciplined process that educators and school teams can use when they wish to emulate the crew of the Starship Enterprise and go boldly where no one has gone before. Action research invites you to explore creative ways to achieve difficult things that, in all likelihood, have yet to be accomplished. As Ronald Heifetz and Marty Linsky (2002) point out, significant performance improvement comes through purposefully addressing adaptive challenges—challenges with no known solution, challenges that cause us to experiment, discover, adjust, and adapt.

Shared Vision Defined

A shared vision accompanied by clear goals is widely accepted as essential if a school or district wishes to achieve or advance the goal of universal student success (Townsend, 2007), yet disagreement remains on what exactly constitutes a shared vision.

In this book, *shared vision* refers to a robust, collective image of a future state where our hopes and dreams have been realized. Shared visions are realized through focused efforts at achieving a specified set of goals. To produce universal student success, goals must be clear and unambiguous. Most people familiar with the literature on professional learning communities are aware of SMART goals. A SMART goal is one that is *S*trategic and *S*pecific, *M*easurable, *A*ttainable, *R*ealistic, and *T*ime-bound (Conzemius & O'Neill, 2002). The construction of high-quality SMART goals is important for fostering quality instruction and school improvement.

Basically, goals are no more than a description of a result, as yet unattained, that you desire to achieve. The reason Habit of Inquiry 1 is so essential for educational architects conducting collaborative action research is that vivid high-quality goals allow you to engage in the backwards planning process—a process that has been shown effective for both students and teachers (Guskey, 2001).

Backwards Planning

Kristi Johnson Smith (2006), a high school teacher from North Carolina, described a recent teaching episode this way (p. 259):

> I thought the day was a success.
>
> I was exhausted, but elated. For the first time ever, I had spent an entire day in my classroom without once seeing a student asleep (bad) or out of control (worse). Perhaps I had finally discovered the real key to managing a classroom. Certainly it was that. But it was also about making the lessons engaging! Instead of just talking about the material, my students had explored it! They had done activity after activity, and I had learned an incredibly important lesson: If I put more energy into making my classroom interesting, I could expend less energy pleading with my kids to stay alert and on task.
>
> One for the "win" column?
>
> Not quite.
>
> The next day, my students struggled to build on that knowledge, and I realized that my activities, while engaging, hadn't really focused on what my students needed to know. I had lost sight of their learning objectives in the midst of my planning. I had gotten so excited about what we could do that I had forgotten to think about what they should learn.

This experience illustrated for Smith the importance of what Grant Wiggins and Jay McTighe (1998) have popularized as backwards planning. Traditional forms of educational planning follow a sequence much like the construction of a house. First you pour a foundation, then you frame the first floor, the second floor, and so on. In backwards planning, however, you follow another sequence—not the one used to construct the house, but the process used by the architect in conceiving. Before thinking about the foundation or the framing, the architect likely reflected on the end result. "What do I want this house to look like, how big should it be, and what special attributes should it have?" With that image firmly in mind, the architect could create drawings that detailed precisely how the house would look when finished. Only then was it time to prepare the blueprints and specifications.

For us as educational architects, backwards planning begins with the development of the same type of clear picture. In our case, it is a vision of where we hope our students will end up. However, knowing what we want to see accomplished and where we want to end up are not enough. To be successful, we still need to answer a few additional questions before we can move more deeply into the planning cycle.

What Is the Context?

Before setting specific goals and proceeding with the development of a detailed theory of action, we need to take full stock of the context in which we are working. All professionals need to know the current status of their clients as well as the specific circumstances they face. The architect needs to know, for example, all about the site—its contours, soil conditions, exposure to sunlight, and zoning rules, as well as the characteristics of the neighborhood and the client's budget. As educational architects the type of contextual factors we may want to consider include our students' attitudes toward the subject, their past performance, parental support, and classroom climate. Understanding the context provides these professionals with insights into how to go about the work.

What Will Success Look Like?

Whenever a PLC team embarks on a significant program improvement initiative, it must articulate an unambiguous shared vision of program success. This is done by generating an answer to a foundational question: "If this initiative results in the realization of our dreams, what will success look like?"

For example, if we are working on an initiative designed to help students write a persuasive essay, we will want to know exactly what an outstanding persuasive essay should contain, how it should read, and how it will affect the reader. If we are working on a character education program, we will need to ask ourselves what attributes are found in graduates with strong character and what we might observe such individuals doing in relation to others. If we are working on helping students understand the concept of ratio, we might ask what understanding ratio means, what a student who understood the concept of ratio would be able to do, and how we would know if a student fully understood the concept of ratio.

The backwards planning process presumes everyone involved (the team, grade level, department, faculty) is pursuing an identical vision. Some might argue that expecting everyone to be committed to the same vision is a restriction on academic freedom. As you proceed through this book, you will see that I am a strong advocate of academic freedom. I believe that empowering classroom teachers to engage in innovative educational architecture and creatively solve nonroutine problems is an essential ingredient of any truly effective school. However, academic freedom doesn't begin until:

- A shared vision has been created.

- The shared vision has been ratified by those charged with carrying it out.

- A set of clear performance targets has been established.

Is There Collective Autonomy?

Carl Glickman (1993) coined the phrase *collective autonomy* to describe a key characteristic of effective schools. This phrase, which at first appears to be an oxymoron, is actually a term of art. Glickman (2002) asserts that our "aim is always toward more individual autonomy for achieving collective learning goals" (p. 104). In an effective school, the shared vision, goals, and achievement targets result from a collaborative process through which goals are ultimately ratified by the faculty. There must be consensus regarding the priority school goals. Someone who does not subscribe to the goals of an enterprise can't be very effective working in that enterprise. This is true in all professions, and it makes sense. It is a fair bet that all cardiologists concur on the attributes of a healthy adult heart and all structural engineers concur on the elements of a stable bridge. What enables the successful professional to provide appropriate and creative service for each unique client is not the freedom to choose an idiosyncratic vision, but the autonomy to design creative ways to realize the shared vision. This autonomy aspect of collective autonomy will be discussed at length in the next chapter.

PLC teams should avoid embarking on an improvement initiative until the team has achieved consensus on its program's shared vision and goals. If you find that members of your team are at odds over key elements of the vision, this means more time must be invested in the vision-setting process.

The Shared-Vision Process at Work

It is now time to work on Habit of Inquiry 1, Clarifying a Shared Vision for Success. This habit is made up of three sequential phases:

1. Articulating the shared vision

2. Identifying the achievement targets

3. Establishing assessment criteria

Articulating the Shared Vision

It has been well established by sports psychologists that you can learn to execute a new and difficult performance far more quickly and efficiently by visualizing its completion in your mind's eye (Martin, Moritz, & Hall, 1999). For this to work, it is critical that you see the envisioned act clearly, with a sharp focus. If the picture in your mind's eye is fuzzy, you risk missing the mark. Similarly, when articulating shared visions of student success, our statements must be precise, unambiguous, and visual.

Authors of fiction are good at clarifying visions for their readers. If we were to select ten random adults to read a well-written book's first chapter—in which the author introduces the protagonist and antagonist and sets the scene—and then ask the readers to close their eyes and visualize the main characters, it is likely they will all see a similar picture. To successfully implement Habit of Inquiry 1, Clarifying a Shared Vision for Success, we want to strive for this same level of clarity.

Often, this is not the level of precision you see with goals established in schools. Take, for example, these elementary school goals (taken from highly regarded schools):

- Promote high academic achievement among all learners.

- Emphasize student-focused instruction appropriate to students' different needs and learning styles.

- Support high levels of learning through coordinated expectations and assessment.

Or these district goals:

- Improve curricular system and instructional practices to challenge every student.

- Provide college readiness and postsecondary preparation for all students.

- Ensure high expectations and support for all students.

All of these goals are virtuous, but are they clear enough? If we asked ten volunteer educators to close their eyes and imagine any of them being accomplished, and later asked them to describe what they were seeing, we would likely get ten fundamentally different scenarios. Yet if we asked ten random cardiologists to describe for us the appearance of a properly functioning aortic valve, all of them would paint a nearly identical picture. When engaged in vision setting, we should strive for the same precision achieved by those cardiologists.

It is critically important, prior to commencing your action research, to articulate a clear vision of a successful outcome by drafting a scenario of success. The following specific exercises were designed to help you and your PLC team create a precise shared vision of success.

Drafting a Scenario of Success

Scenario writing is a process that any PLC team can employ. The steps consist of individual reflective writing and deconstructing that writing. This process invites maximum input from every member of your team, and for this reason is best completed during dedicated time at a PLC meeting. It should take no more than one and one-half hours to complete; however, it doesn't need to be completed in one sitting.

Step 1: Individual reflective writing. Using a common prompt, each person on the PLC team is given fifteen to thirty minutes of quiet time to reflect on precisely what would constitute outstanding performance in the team's focus area. The two Reflective Writing Prompts (pages 24–25 and online at **go.solution-tree.com/plcbooks**) are examples of forms created for this purpose.

Step 2: Deconstruction of personal scenarios of success. The reflective writing pieces that emerge from step 1 should be accurate verbal depictions of what success will ultimately look and feel like, as perceived by the individual members of your PLC team. Before continuing to the next step, it is important to ascertain if, in fact, these verbal images succeeded in accurately communicating the visions of their authors. This is done by having each person read aloud the success scenario he or she drafted, while the other PLC members attempt to identify and name each achievement target present in the scenario. Use the Target Identification Form (page 26) for this exercise.

After each member has had a chance to present his or her scenario of success, the completed Target Identification Forms are returned to the presenters. In a perfect world, where we all are able to write eloquently and are totally in tune with our own thinking, each list of targets would be identical and would match perfectly with the list generated by the author. But the world is rarely that perfect. Let's presume we are members of a middle-school language arts team and our shared vision involved developing self-confident, persuasive public speakers by the end of eighth grade. Our team decided that we would take twenty minutes and write up our visions using Reflective Writing Prompt 2 (page 25). The scenario of success I could have written and shared with my team members might read like the following:

> Johnny approached the podium at the front of the classroom with a broad smile on his face and a stack of note cards. He opened his remarks by telling us of the need for a series of alcohol- and drug-free events for youth in our community. He went on to explore three or four different community problems that he felt resulted from the absence of healthy social alternatives for local youth. He made the argument that bad behavior is the result of too much unstructured idle time on the weekends. He went on to tell us how a system of high-interest, Friday- and Saturday-night supervised events would provide benefits for local youth and mitigate the attractiveness of antisocial behavior such as drinking and drugs. He concluded with a plea to our commitment to youth. He claimed that the future of the next generation is in our hands. He closed by saying we could close our eyes and "wish for the best or choose to be proactive in planning safe and fun free-time activities for our youth."

Identifying the Achievement Targets

After my peers reviewed my scenario of success and filled out the Target Identification Forms and I looked over their lists, I noticed that all six of my teammates identified the same items. Specifically, everyone noted that Johnny had shown evidence of hitting these achievement targets:

- Creating and presenting a logical thesis

- Providing evidence in support of his thesis

- Engaging his audience

Since each of my peers identified the same achievement targets embedded in my scenario, it is a fair bet that I had adequately addressed those targets. However, that wasn't the whole story. Two of my six colleagues reported hearing an additional target in my narrative. They both heard:

- Discussing alternative perspectives

This was very helpful information. It also pointed out a problem. First, let's assume that I had intended my personal vision to include discussing alternative perspectives. The fact that four colleagues missed seeing it in my written scenario of success indicates that I hadn't made that achievement target nearly as clear as I should have. If my scenario had been accepted as the team's shared vision, a colleague might easily have overlooked the critical feature of discussing alternative perspectives while thinking he or she was pursuing the vision we had all agreed upon. Fortunately, I was able to easily remedy the problem by editing my scenario and adding an example of Johnny discussing alternative perspectives.

Getting peer feedback improved my original scenario of success, but the step of vision deconstruction will not be complete until I do one more thing. I need to look at the feedback from my colleagues and ask myself if there are other elements of "self-confident, persuasive public speaking" that I value that failed to appear on anyone's list. This is often the case. Many times the things we value most get overlooked in our initial narrative writing simply because we take them for granted. For example, it may be very important to me that students make use of metaphor and analogy in their speeches. Additionally, I may want my students to develop a sense of empowerment as a result of becoming proficient with public speaking. But none of my colleagues identified those achievement targets as present in my scenario. As a result, I will need to further edit it to ensure that it includes all the attributes I value.

Scenario deconstruction is complete once each PLC team member possesses a completed personal narrative, accompanied by a list of achievement targets that he or she believes accurately reflect student success with this goal. Now it's time to use these personal narratives to build the shared vision.

Create a Target Comparison Worksheet similar to the one illustrated in figure 1.1 (page 18). On page 27, you will find a blank version of this worksheet. In the left-hand column, list every achievement target that was identified in the final version of any member's scenario. Across the top, place the names of the PLC team members. Then the team members individually ask themselves if they believe that each identified target (those listed on the vertical axis) is critical to achieving the overall goal. A checkmark is placed by each attribute or target that a team member deems critical for achievement of the goal.

Targets (from written scenarios)	Juan	Marcia	Jeff	Maryann	Ralph
Clear Thesis	X	X	X	X	X
Ample Evidence	X	X	X	X	X
Alternative Perspectives	X		X	X	
Use of Analogy and Metaphor	X		X	X	
Clear Proposal	X	X	X	X	X
Strong Conclusion	X	X	X	X	X
Audience Engagement	X	X	X	X	X

Figure 1.1: Target comparison worksheet.

Once the Target Comparison Worksheet has been filled out, the team is ready to begin drafting its shared vision. This is a group writing exercise. For each target, your team will already have numerous good examples to consider (the individual pieces of reflective writing). If all the team members had not checked a particular target on the worksheet, the group should discuss the importance of that particular target to the realization of the overall goal. The team should deliberate on these questions, "Is this target truly essential for universal student success?" and "Is this target a part of our team's shared vision of student proficiency with this goal?" Then, based upon those deliberations, the target will either be included or omitted from the team's shared scenario of success.

The scenario process is considered finished once a shared scenario has been developed, along with an agreed-upon list of targets. The following illustrates how my PLC team's completed scenario of success on persuasive public speaking might read and includes the team's list of component achievement targets:

> Johnny approached the podium in the front of the classroom with a broad smile on his face and a stack of note cards. He began by sharing a story about a community in which every weekend was filled with healthy, supervised activities for youth. He asked his audience to share times when they were productively engaged in healthful weekend activities as middle-school youth.
>
> He then spoke to tell us in graphic detail about the temptations that were facing youth in our community and how these were resulting in many youth making unhealthy choices. He shared how every weekend he and his peers faced pressure to attend unsupervised parties where alcohol was readily available.

He argued that the self-destructive behavior of local youth wasn't because they were "bad kids," but because there were so few constructive options. He asserted, "If kids had a choice of activities on weekends and some of those activities were interesting, fun, and supervised, I guarantee that students from our school would choose these 'safer' activities."

Johnny shared a proposal for how, through a combined effort of the PTA and the local churches, the community could create high-interest events that would be held virtually every Friday and Saturday night. He assured us that his proposal would not overburden any one agency and would provide youth with continuity and a positive outlet for their energy. He laid out several strategies to raise money to ensure that no student would be unable to attend an activity due to cost considerations.

Johnny acknowledged that not everyone would agree with his proposal. He said some adults in our community argue that it's up to the parents to find safe activities for their students over the weekends and that there already were enough positive outlets for youth who desired them. He countered these arguments by saying that the current situation results in high rates of alcohol abuse and delinquency by area youth and it isn't fair to hold students hostage to the values of their parents. He ended his talk by sharing that, in his opinion, this issue wasn't so much an issue of money or expertise as one of commitment. He said, "If the adults care enough and are willing to back up their concern with action, our community can become a safe place for youth." It was, in his words, "a matter of will." When Johnny concluded his speech, his audience stood and applauded.

Specific achievement targets:

- Clear thesis

- Evidence in support of thesis

- Alternative perspectives

- Use of analogy and metaphor

- Clear proposal

- Strong conclusion

- Audience engagement

Establishing Assessment Criteria

One goal of professional learning communities should be nurturing a culture of collective autonomy. Building shared vision is part of the process of producing such a culture, but it is only a start. In fact, we are not quite finished developing the "collective" aspect of collective autonomy. While it is critically important that everyone share an unambiguous picture of success, full mastery of Habit of Inquiry 1, Clarifying a Shared Vision for Success, requires one additional step. Simply knowing what a quality performance looks like doesn't provide a sufficient foundation for the exercise of creative educational architecture. That requires a set of clear and agreed-upon assessment criteria.

Leadership Note

Whenever teams of faculty members or the faculty as a whole reach consensus on a shared vision, that vision must be shared with the entire school community. It is always easier to hit a target that you can see clearly. Therefore, everyone who might play a role in producing the desired outcome should be fully cognizant of the shared vision, with all its nuances.

Some strategies to communicate PLC team shared visions as a normal part of the school routine are:

- Creating a dedicated time at faculty meetings when PLC teams can share their scenarios of success

- Creating a dedicated space on the school's website for sharing and displaying the scenarios

- Periodically publishing all of the adopted scenarios of success in a booklet available for student, staff, and parental review

Achievement Targets as Dependent Variables

Every achievement target delineated in the final PLC team scenario of success is the equivalent of what researchers call a *dependent variable*. A dependent variable is a change in outcome that someone wishes to produce. When I am working on getting physically fit, my weight, resting heart rate, and body fat index are all dependent variables. Measuring changes in my performance on each of the identified dependent variables enables me to monitor the success of my fitness program. Likewise, if I am creating a novel way to effect an improvement in student performance on a shared PLC team goal, I will want to measure changes on each dependent variable that our team felt influenced student success with our goal. Therefore, before we can consider ourselves finished with our work on Habit of Inquiry 1, our team must establish a set of unambiguous assessment criteria for each dependent variable, or achievement target.

This can be easily accomplished by developing what researchers call a *graphical rating scale* for each goal being pursued. The graphical rating scales we will be using are assessment rubrics with behavioral anchors. You can easily build a single rating scale for a program goal with multiple targets. This is accomplished by creating a row on the rubric for the assessment of each achievement target or dependent variable. The Rating Scale for Persuasive Public Speaking (fig. 1.2) shows a portion of a hypothetical rating scale developed for the use of the middle-school PLC team working on the goal of creating self-confident, persuasive public speakers.

Rubrics may contain as many columns as the team feels are needed, so long as there are unambiguous distinctions between the behaviors or performances described in each column.

Target	1 Basic	2 Emerging	3 Developing	4 Proficient	5 Fluent
Clear Thesis	A thesis is stated.	A thesis is stated clearly.	A clear and complete thesis is articulated.	A complete and clear thesis is articulated and referenced throughout the text.	A complete and clear thesis is articulated, and the entire presentation is structured in support of the thesis.
Evidence	Something is said in support of the thesis.	Some evidence is cited as a rationale for supporting the thesis.	Multiple pieces of evidence are cited in support of the thesis.	Multiple pieces of evidence supportive of the thesis are presented in a convincing manner.	Multiple pieces of evidence are employed strategically to make a powerful case in support of the thesis.
Alternative Perspectives	It is acknowledged that some people dispute the thesis.	A rationale is given why some people might not support the thesis.	The logic behind differing positions on the thesis is discussed and refuted.	The logic behind differing positions on the thesis is discussed, and evidence is provided for their rejection.	All reasonable arguments against the thesis are made, discussed, and refuted with logic and evidence.

Figure 1.2: Rating scale for persuasive public speaking.

To be as useful as possible for action research, the graphical rating scale should also adhere to a set of basic guidelines, as follows:

1. **Midpoint (developing).** The rating scale should have a midpoint, which means that whenever possible, scales should have an odd number of columns—for example, three, five, or seven—so that one of the columns is in the middle. This midpoint indicates work that would be considered good performance for students of this age. We might think of it as equivalent to grade-level performance on this target. It is a level of work you would expect from a student who was making adequate progress and was developmentally prepared for the work ahead.

2. **Lowest score (basic).** The bottom score on the scale is the minimal level of performance a student might possibly demonstrate. This performance should not be

confused with incompetence or failure. Rather, the bottom score is evidence of movement toward mastery, if only by a baby step.

3. **Highest score (fluent).** The top score is reserved for a level of performance that is truly extraordinary. The degree of mastery this score represents is so special that it is hard to imagine a student ever doing better.

The reason for stretching our rating scales from minimal competence to extraordinary performance is to maximize the rating scale's value for the educational architect. When assessing and planning instruction for individual students, we need data that are sensitive enough to alert us to even the most subtle movement along a continuum. Finally, we want to set the top end of the scale high enough so that it can capture and report on the incremental growth of our very best students.

Building Rating Scales at a PLC Meeting

A PLC team can easily construct a shared rating scale by following these eight steps:

1. **Draw the matrix on chart paper.** Tape a six-foot sheet of chart paper to the wall. Draw the Rating Scale Worksheet matrix (page 28) on the chart paper.

2. **Distribute sticky pads.** Give each team member his or her own pad of sticky notes, using a different color for each person.

3. **Review the achievement targets.** Starting with the first target, the team reminds itself (if necessary, by rereading the shared scenario of success) of what is meant by each achievement target.

4. **Place team members' ideas of hitting targets on the matrix.** Each team member jots down on a sticky note one observable student demonstration of hitting each achievement target at the developing level. Members then place the sticky notes in the middle column of the appropriate row of the matrix for each achievement target.

5. **Discuss the sticky notes.** The group discusses the sticky notes and decides which observable behaviors best fit the team's view of developing performance on this target.

6. **Repeat steps 1–5 for columns 1 and 5.** The group repeats steps 1–5, first for the emerging column and then for the fluent column.

7. **Repeat steps 1–5 for columns 2 and 4.** As a group, team members decide which intermediate behaviors fall between the emerging, developing, and fluent ratings.

8. **Ratify the completed scale.** The group then reviews and discusses the completed rating scale. Once group members reach agreement, they should formally ratify their rating scale(s). Ratification must be by consensus. The visioning process isn't complete until there is unanimous agreement that the collaboratively developed rating scale (that is, the agreed-upon assessment criteria) is an accurate representation of the group's goals and the range of student performance the team expects to observe.

Leadership Note

It is in everyone's interest that the criteria by which student success will be determined is as public as possible. Furthermore, the process of setting shared visions, targets, and assessment criteria is hard work, for which participants deserve recognition. For these and other reasons, it is important to be transparent about assessment criteria. Some of the ways leadership can accomplish this include:

- Creating a dedicated time at faculty meetings for PLC teams to share their assessment rating scales

- Establishing a dedicated space on the school's website for sharing the assessment rating scales being developed and used by the school's PLC teams

- Periodically publishing the rating scales in a booklet available around the school for student, staff, and parental review

Conclusion

Once shared visions have been fully clarified and articulated, a PLC team is well on its way to achieving the collective aspect of collective autonomy. Furthermore, the evidence from research on curriculum alignment suggests that if teachers collaborated only on the development of shared visions, goals, and assessment criteria, that in itself would positively influence student performance. There is no overstating the importance of achieving clarity regarding where we are going and what we want to achieve. It allows teachers to keep their eye on the destination and focus their finite time and energy. For students, a clearly stated shared vision takes the mystery out of the instructional process, enables them to track their own improvement, and provides them with opportunities to feel genuinely good about themselves as they progress along a developmental continuum.

If producing the shared vision that emerges from Habit 1 was the end of our work, it would likely be beneficial for our students, but the premise of this book is that we can accomplish much, much more. Through the mastery of all five habits of inquiry, we can move ever closer to the elusive goal of universal student success. For a team conducting action research, knowing precisely where you hope to end up is a critical first step; once you have accomplished this, your attention will shift to another question, "How do I get to my destination?" In Habit of Inquiry 2, Articulating Theories of Action, we will answer that question.

Reflective Writing Prompt 1

Name: _____   Date: _____

Please respond to the following prompt with as much descriptive detail as possible. Do your best to use everyday language, avoiding the use of educational jargon.

> *Imagine it is five years from now. Your work with your program or subject area has been successful beyond everyone's wildest dreams. A team of visiting educators recently visited your school and left tremendously impressed with your success. Upon returning home, they reported on their visit at a faculty meeting at their home school. After they shared their enthusiasm for your program, a skeptical colleague asked, "Would you please tell us precisely what it was you observed during your visit that impressed you so much?"*

Write down with as much detail as possible what you heard said in reply.

Reflective Writing Prompt 2

Name: Date:

Please respond to the following prompt with as much descriptive detail as possible. Do your best to use everyday language, avoiding the use of educational jargon.

Imagine it is five years from now, and your program has succeeded beyond your wildest expectations. You are witnessing one of your students presenting an end-of-program exhibition. The student's assignment is to demonstrate his or her proficiency with your subject or focus area. This student is a perfect example of what you had hoped to accomplish. Describe in as much detail as possible what you hear the student saying and observe the student doing for his or her exhibition.

Target Identification Form

Scenario Author:

What specific student learning and which skills did you see demonstrated in this scenario of success? List all the program outcomes, student outcomes, and skills you saw evidence of in this written scenario.

Target Comparison Worksheet

Use this form to compare and contrast the achievement targets that surfaced in the personal visions developed by team members.

There should be one column for each team member. Enter each member's name in the top row. In the left-hand column write a brief description of each identified achievement target (use a separate row for each target).

Each member then indicates with a check mark those achievement targets that appeared in his or her scenario.

Targets (from written scenarios)					

Rating Scale Worksheet

This worksheet was designed to assist in the creation of a graphical rating scale for assessing incremental growth in pursuit of an achievement target. Traits are subcategories of a target. For example, if the target was proficient expository writing, traits might include organization, word choice, mechanics, and so on. The numbered columns are for behavioral descriptions of performance. A fluent (5) performance should be at a level that is truly extraordinary. The middle column, developing (3), should contain a description of performance that meets expectations. The emerging (1) column should contain the most minimal behavior that qualifies as a demonstration of the trait.

Trait	Emerging 1	Basic 2	Developing 3	Proficient 4	Fluent 5

Habit of Inquiry
Articulating
Theories of Action

Hopefully, at this point you and your team have used the scenario-writing process or followed a visioning strategy of your own design and created a clear, shared vision of success. You should also have created an agreed-upon set of assessment criteria that can be used to monitor progress, as you and your students take action toward realizing your shared vision. By doing these two things, you have demonstrated your skills with Habit of Inquiry 1, Clarifying a Shared Vision for Success. In reality, you are practicing Habit 1 whenever you find yourself pausing before instruction to verbally clarify to yourself or your colleagues precisely what you are seeking to accomplish and the criteria you will use to determine your progress.

Beyond the practical benefits that come from having common expectations, a deep sense of professional satisfaction comes from working as a group to collaboratively pinpoint precisely what the team wishes to see accomplished. As a PLC team, you should now be feeling very good about your work with Habit 1 and the consensus you have achieved on the aims of your program.

Habit of Inquiry 2, Articulating Theories of Action, may be the most important, intellectually challenging, and creative aspect of the entire collaborative action research process. Because of the work you've already accomplished, you should now be able to confidently tell colleagues, students, and parents exactly what it is you want to see achieved and how you will measure and monitor progress toward universal proficiency. This is a significant accomplishment, as it eliminates uncertainty for the learner and provides focus for the teacher.

But precision about outcomes cannot obscure a powerful truth: in all likelihood, you and your team don't yet know, with any degree of certainty, *how* to achieve universal success on the targets you've identified. Why do I say this? To begin with, you would not have selected a goal as the focus for your collaborative action research if you felt you were already realizing it. As busy educators, we tend to focus our program improvement energies on whatever hasn't been working as well as we would have hoped. But, if we are working in an area where student performance has been disappointing, all things being equal, why should we expect different results this time around?

Clearly, if we want fundamentally different results from our efforts, we will need to explore fundamentally different approaches. Heifetz and Linsky (2002) describe this type of change as an *adaptive challenge*. Habit of Inquiry 2, Articulating Theories of Action, is where the action research process requires you to immerse yourself deeply in the creative and innovative work of the educational architect.

Macro- and Micro-Level Projects

In a true professional learning community, action research projects are happening all the time. Different teams will utilize the collaborative action research process for a variety of purposes. Some projects will be focused on the achievement of schoolwide or programwide goals, while others (generally grade-level or departmental teams) will be focused on designing classroom-level improvements. As we proceed, we will refer to those two categories of projects as macro-level (school and program) initiatives and micro-level (classroom) initiatives.

When working at the macro level, the end product of a team's work on theory development results in a theory of action that articulates the steps to be followed either by the staff of a specific program or by the entire faculty as they collaboratively work to realize the shared vision. Shared visions at the macro level can be as broad as a schoolwide perspective on the attributes of an ideal graduate or as narrow as a program vision as captured and reported in an adopted PLC team scenario (pages 18–19).

By contrast, micro-level projects will generally focus on helping an identified group of students to achieve success with a particular achievement target (usually a subcomponent of either a schoolwide vision or a PLC team's adopted scenario of success). In either case, the basic process for theory development is similar in both macro and micro level projects. The few process differences pertain to the scope of the work undertaken and the nature of the collaboration involved.

A Macro-Level Project

We will begin with an illustration of a team applying the theory articulation process at the macro (schoolwide) level—specifically, in designing an initiative aimed at helping the student body to acquire positive character traits. Later, we will see how this theory-building process can be modified for use by individuals and teams working at the micro level for interventions designed to improve individual student performance on classroom-based achievement targets.

Identifying the Independent Variables

The theory-building process begins by reconnecting with the shared vision. Take a few moments to reread the scenario you developed during the first stage of the collaborative action research process (or reread any other document that clearly articulates your shared vision). As you recall, your scenario wasn't considered complete until it was ratified as accurate and clear by all members of the PLC team. Operationally, being clear meant that each team member, when closing his or her eyes and imagining a successful student, would see the same image.

In the last chapter, we introduced the idea of the dependent variable. The dependent variable is what you hope to see changed as a result of one's actions. The program goal we will now be exploring encompasses two dependent variables:

1. The creation of the comprehensive character education program

2. The development of graduates with positive character traits

For this example, let's assume the shared school vision included a fully implemented, comprehensive character education program that produced universal student success on a variety of measures of character. Let's also assume assessment criteria have been established (graphical rating scales) for both of the dependent variables. The critical question for us as educational architects is how to go about achieving success on these two dependent variables. We know program and student success won't occur by accident. If there is to be a change in either of the dependent variables, it will be because some significant actions occurred. The array of actions and phenomena that lead to success on a dependent variable are called the *independent variables*. For example, if my vision for myself is that I become a fit and healthy adult, then my level of fitness and my physical well-being are my dependent variables. There are numerous independent variables that would likely have an impact on my dependent variables, including:

*   Managing my calorie intake

*   Exercising regularly

*   Eating a healthy diet

*   Avoiding intoxicants and other bodily pollutants

*   Consulting and following my doctor's advice

To realize my fitness goals, the set of independent variables I will focus on needs to be both powerful and comprehensive. Ultimately, my success will depend on how well I attend to each of them.

Determining the Salience of the Independent Variables

What follows is a fun, three-step process that assists PLC teams in identifying and assessing the particular independent variables they believe must be addressed if they are to achieve universal student success on their priority goals.

1. **Brainstorm individually.** After reading through the ratified scenario (or otherwise reflecting on the shared vision), each member of the team brainstorms, on a separate sheet of paper, every significant phenomena, variable, or issue that he or she believes must be attended to if the shared vision is to be realized. When working on realizing a schoolwide or programwide vision, the achievement targets that your team identified

at the shared vision–setting stage will likely appear as independent variables on everyone's list. This makes sense, since those were the achievement targets that had been identified as prerequisite for realizing the shared vision.

However, the brainstorming process shouldn't end with the identification of the essential achievement targets. There will inevitably be other factors that you feel are critical to achieving your goals. For example, if I were working as part of a team pursuing the target of developing a comprehensive character education program, I might regard the following phenomena, factors, variables, or issues as critical for achieving our goal:

- Community service

- Recognizing and appreciating diversity

- Staff development

- School policy regarding character education

- Common core values

- School governance

2. **Expand the list.** Once every member of the group has brainstormed a personal list of independent variables, the lists are shared and discussed. Invariably, some items will occur to some members and not to others. The group should discuss these discrepancies and attempt to come up with a composite list that everyone can agree to. The criterion for placing an item on the team's composite list is that the particular phenomena, factor, or issue is deemed to be so important that it *must* be addressed if *all* students are to realize the shared vision.

The two words in italics are critical. Some actions may be valuable and helpful, yet not be deemed as essential for success. Those items don't belong on the final list. Other actions will appear so critical that without them it seems certain some students won't succeed. Those items should remain on the team's list of independent variables. Sometimes it will be necessary to repeat the brainstorming process several times until the team feels it has generated a set of independent variables comprehensive enough to produce universal success with its goal.

Occasionally, the group will find itself unable to reach consensus on a set of critical independent variables. If that happens with your group, look upon this disagreement as an opportunity rather than a problem. Divergent views on the specific actions necessary for success can be something to celebrate. After all, if the answer to the particular issue you have decided to address was easy, simple, or straightforward, your team would have already solved it, your students would all be succeeding, and all would be well with the world. Since, by definition, a satisfactory answer to the challenge you are pursuing has proven elusive, considering multiple perspectives may be in your team's collective best interest. If it turns out that your group can't agree on a single list of independent variables, it is okay to proceed to step 3 with alternative sets of independent variables.

3. **Assess the salience of the independent variables.** Make a copy of the Independent Variable Assessment Form (page 50) for each member of your team. Ask team members to write down those independent variables they believe belong on the final list. Even when everyone has already agreed on a single composite list, each team member should individually complete an Independent Variable Assessment Form. Having listed all the key independent variables, each team member then asks this question of each item on his or her list: "How important is this particular factor, phenomena, or variable to the achievement of universal success on this target?"

Based upon his or her response to that question, each person writes on his or her copy of the Independent Variable Assessment Form a percentage reflecting his or her perception of the relative importance of that variable for ensuring universal success on the target. The total percentages awarded by each person must add up to one hundred.

Once each member has assigned percentages to his or her list of independent variables, he or she should draw a pie graph displaying the percentages in the space at the bottom of the form. The pie graphs that emerge at this point are visual depictions of what that member believes will be required to achieve universal success on this target—in other words, the graphs are the beginning of that team member's theory of action for this target. Figure 2.1 illustrates my perspective on what will be needed to realize my school's goal of developing a comprehensive character education program. Pie graphs illustrating the relative salience of inferred independent variables have been referred to as *priority pies* (Sagor, 1992a, 2000, 2005).

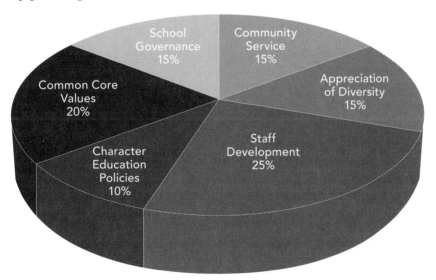

Figure 2.1: Priority pie for a comprehensive character education program.

Once each member has completed a drawing of a priority pie, the team convenes once again to share, discuss, and deliberate over these different representations of variable salience. Often a team will quickly coalesce around one of the priority pies. If that happens, the team is able to say with a high degree of confidence:

We have met and considered what we feel will be required to achieve universal success with this goal. After careful consideration, it is our shared perspective that universal student success will be dependent on our ability to appropriately attend to a specific set of factors, phenomena, and variables. While we consider each of these factors, phenomena, and variables to be important, in our opinion, some will have a greater influence on our ultimate success than others. The following pie graph and percentages reflect our assessment of the relative importance of these factors, phenomena, or variables.

Should the team be unable to agree on a single set of independent variables, then it should produce multiple priority pies. When that occurs, the team is able to declare:

After careful consideration, it has become clear that the members of our team hold divergent views on what will be required to produce universal success with this target. Therefore, we have generated several alternative perspectives for the faculty [community] to consider regarding what will be required to produce universal success.

Leadership Note

One important way to help the professionals working in your school internalize Habit of Inquiry 2 is to make the preparation and sharing of priority pies a regular part of the discourse of the learning community. A strategy for accomplishing this is to routinely construct priority pies whenever a new school or program goal is proposed or discussed. Whenever an individual or group suggests pursuing something, the first question leadership should ask is, "What do you think it will take for us to realize this goal?" At this point, the person proposing the goal should pause and construct a tentative priority pie for sharing with his or her colleagues.

Priority pies are rarely complete or accurate the first time they are drafted. Frequently, they are made up of educated suppositions, which will be revised after further discussion. Nevertheless, when leadership requests that a pie be constructed and shared prior to commencing deliberations, it reinforces the view that significant growth rarely happens by accident and that nothing changes without focused attention to a specified set of underlying phenomena. Although we intuitively know this to be the case, the time pressure we are under often results in moving from problem identification to a proposal without stopping to take stock of the relevant independent variables. Using priority pies as an integral part of a school's planning process will help ensure that critical variables are not overlooked.

Lastly, once a schoolwide initiative is underway, the priority pie that informed that initiative should be prominently posted and made available to all interested parties.

Building the Visual Theory of Action

We have been using architecture as a metaphor for collaborative inquiry, but we might also think of the action research process as a journey. We could say that thus far we have created a basic itinerary for this journey. In Habit of Inquiry 1, you clarified what a satisfactory journey would be (the shared vision captured in your scenario). The priority pies you developed can be seen as representing the cities you hope to visit on your trip. Creating this type of broad-brush itinerary is an essential first step for any traveler, but it is far from the detailed itinerary you will later need, and it certainly isn't detailed enough to provide an adequate plan for attacking an adaptive school or program challenge. You will need more to guide your school improvement journey than a sliced-up priority pie.

The theory of action captured on your pie graph is what could be called an *emergent theory*. It is a rough outline of what lies ahead for you, your colleagues, and your students. Now it is time to move from that rough outline to a more elaborate one, with enough detail to guide your expedition. The next stage in the process is therefore the construction of a visual plan— what we will be referring to as a visual theory of action. This visual plan will illustrate the specific route(s) you need to take to realize your shared vision or hit your achievement targets. Designing a visual theory of action is a creative and dynamic planning process. Frequently, researchers refer to visual theories of action as *graphic reconstructions*. Your visual theory of action, or graphic reconstruction, will outline how you can move from the present situation to the desired outcome, specifically the realization of your shared vision.

Anytime you work on the design of schoolwide or programwide (macro-level) improvement, the planning process used should be maximally inclusive. Every professional who is expected to be working on the project (or may at some point contribute toward the realization of the goal) should have input into the development of the theory that will ultimately direct the group's collective actions.

Most visual theories of action created by action researchers look something like a cross between a flowchart and a web, or mind map. They graphically illustrate the relationships between the factors, phenomena, and variables that the team believes will come into play as they, their colleagues, and their students pursue the identified target. Like a good roadmap, a visual theory of action provides the specific direction needed as one journeys over untraveled terrain to a foreign destination. Figure 2.2 (page 36) shows a visual theory of action for a comprehensive character development program for use by a middle school.

You will notice that the school's SMART goals are included at the bottom of this graphic. These are the goals that, once achieved, will constitute the realization of the schoolwide vision. You will also notice that the graphic references the specific actions to be taken (such as recognition programs, classroom meetings, and peer tutoring), as well as the anticipated barriers that will need to be overcome (such as traditions, academic status, and social status).

The actual process of building a visual theory of action for a macro-level project can be accomplished in ten steps that can take one to two hours.

1. **Assemble the necessary materials.** Obtain a big sheet of chart paper that can be laid across a table or posted on a wall, so that the entire team can gather around and work together. You will also need felt-tip pens and several pads of different-colored sticky notes.

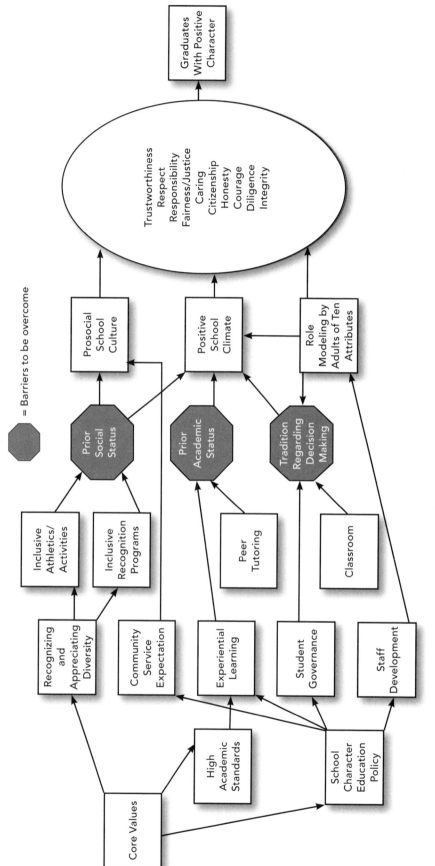

SMART Goals:
- Prosocial behavior will increase consistently, as measured by a steady reduction in disciplinary referrals and incidents.
- Students will accept greater personal responsibility, as evidenced by continuous increases in assignment completion, grades, and recognitions awarded for responsible behavior.

Figure 2.2: Visual theory of action for a character education program.

2. **Clarify the shared vision or target.** As a group, take a moment to review what precisely you are hoping to accomplish through this initiative. This may require reviewing the scenario of success you adopted or other documentation that articulates your shared vision.

3. **Brainstorm individually.** Using the Visual Theory of Action Planning Form (page 51), each PLC team member individually brainstorms each action, factor, phenomena, or variable that he or she feels might affect success in realizing the shared vision or hitting the agreed-upon target. Additionally, each team member brainstorms barriers that he or she suspects have the potential to hinder success.

   Note that when you constructed the priority pies, you only considered the essential variables. When using the Visual Theory of Action Planning Form, include those same essential variables as well as other relevant activities or actions that you believe should be part of the implementation plan.

4. **Share the lists.** In a group setting, each member of the team reports the specific actions, factors, phenomena, and barriers that appeared on his or her individual lists. The purpose of this sharing is to:

   - Clarify and consolidate ideas.

   - Stimulate the generation of additional factors or variables that may have been overlooked.

   - Begin collaborative problem solving for overcoming anticipated barriers.

5. **Orient the graphic.** On the extreme right side of the chart paper, place a note saying "Desired Outcome." This is where you and your students will end up if your plan works perfectly and all the students meet all your goals, hit all your targets, and realize your shared vision. The extreme left side represents the things you currently have in place. In the middle of the poster paper, place sticky notes representing each of the barriers, obstacles, or anticipated problems that are likely to be encountered as you travel from the current condition to "Desired Outcome."

6. **Brainstorm actions, factors, phenomena, and variables (as a group).** Using the lists generated in step 3 and shared in step 4, create a deck of sticky notes. This is done by placing every single action, factor, phenomena, or variable that appeared on any member's list onto a separate sticky note. Some groups choose to color code the sticky notes according to whether they refer to an action, barrier, or outcome.

7. **Perform group action planning.** As a group, place the sticky notes on the poster paper, arranging them in a fashion that clearly displays the steps needed to move from the current situation to "Desired Outcome." Be sure that you have created strategies to overcome any obstacles placed in your path.

8. **Proof the graphic.** Once the team feels its visual theory of action is complete, it should generate a list of the different categories of students who are likely to be engaged with this program, for example:

- Alienated students with poor grades

- Academically able students with high self-esteem

- Academically able students who are loners

Now walk through the visual theory of action in the shoes of a student from each one of the categories you generated. As you take your walk, look for places where the student might be likely to get derailed. If you encounter such a stumbling block, consider as a team how you might creatively design a workaround for this stumbling block.

Upon examination of the original visual theory of action developed for the character development program (fig. 2.2, page 36), you might notice that it reflects the belief that the high engagement that results from experiential learning will be powerful enough to overcome a critical barrier, the stigma of low academic status. When proofing their graphic by walking in the shoes of the historically low-performing students, the team realized that many of those young people would need more than peer tutoring and access to an experiential curriculum if they were to truly start seeing themselves as valued members of the school community. The team realized they needed to design a workaround for this apparent roadblock. After some discussion, they reasoned that by adding two new wrinkles to their comprehensive character education program, historically low-performing students would likely receive the support and encouragement needed to overcome the stigma of their prior academic status.

First, they decided to create a mentoring program in which teachers could demonstrate a special interest in these historically low performers, and they planned to implement an academic coaching program (built on an athletic coaching model). Their thinking was that by adding the twin supports of mentoring and coaching, combined with peer tutoring, the historically low-performing students would be more likely to experience success with the experiential curriculum and therefore develop positive attitudes toward themselves and their community.

Figure 2.3 (page 39) is the modified visual theory of action prepared by the PLC Team incorporating these two newly designed workarounds.

9. **Solicit feedback.** A good visual theory of action is more than a research tool—it is a communication device. To use a sports metaphor, it helps new members of a team understand the plays that are being run. Furthermore, a good visual theory of action can assist students and parents to better understand what is expected of them by making the school processes more coherent and comprehensible. Finally, a functional visual theory of action provides continuous direction for a PLC team as it pushes ahead with its work. For all these reasons, once the PLC team completes the development of its visual theory of action, it is a good idea to ask a set of critical friends to review it. One good way to accomplish this is by scheduling a meeting with another PLC team and presenting your visual theory of action to them. After a brief explanation of your theory,

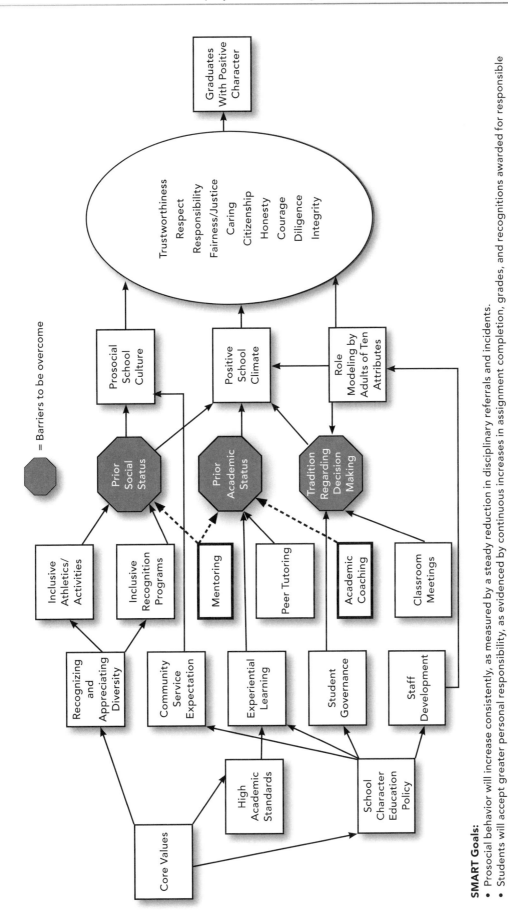

= Barriers to be overcome

SMART Goals:

• Prosocial behavior will increase consistently, as measured by a steady reduction in disciplinary referrals and incidents.

• Students will accept greater personal responsibility, as evidenced by continuous increases in assignment completion, grades, and recognitions awarded for responsible behavior.

Figure 2..3: Modified visual theory of action for a comprehensive character education program.

ask each member of the other team to respond to the first question on the Visual Theory of Action Feedback Form (page 52), "In 150 words or less, explain what is being proposed." Then, each of your critical friends should share what he or she has written.

If the comments from your colleagues show that they captured the essence of what your team was proposing, you will have clear evidence that your graphic is communicating effectively. However, to the extent that your colleagues' responses vary from the team's intentions, it means that further revisions to the visual theory of action will be necessary. When that happens, ask your critical friends to share their answers to the second question on the Visual Theory of Action Feedback Form: "Is there anything that should be added to this theory that will make it more likely to succeed with our students?"

10. **Consider the feedback and revise the graphic.** Meet as a team, review the feedback you received from your critical friends, and make any changes you feel are needed. You are nearly finished. The only remaining step is to write a brief narrative description of your visual theory of action and the dynamic interactions depicted on your graphic. What follows is the description that the PLC team wrote to accompany its character development theory of action (fig. 2.3, page 39):

> Our goal is to have graduates of Sagor Middle School displaying positive character traits. After careful consideration, we have identified ten attributes we believe need to be reinforced with all our students. We believe that these traits can be fostered by a prosocial school culture, a positive school climate, and role modeling by all the adults at school. Experience has told us that there are three barriers that we will need to overcome if we are to succeed with this work: (1) prior student social hierarchies, (2) prior student academic hierarchies, and (3) our traditional way of making decisions.
>
> The heart of our theory is that our existing core values, high academic expectations, and character education policies need to be leveraged so we can overcome the three identified barriers. We believe this will result in a positive evolution of the culture and climate of our school, making it more conducive to character development. Specifically, we need to demonstrate our collective recognition and appreciation of diversity through an inclusive athletic activities program and the development of inclusive recognition programs. Community service needs to become a norm for the entire school community. Instruction should be based on an experiential curriculum model with peer tutoring, mentoring, and academic coaching available to any student who needs it. We will be addressing the encouragement of student voices through an inclusive student governance program and the incorporation of democratic class meetings in every classroom. Finally, staff development will be provided in an effort to assist the faculty in becoming effective role models of the ten character attributes. We expect this effort to result in measurable outcomes—specifically, improved behavior as shown by a reduction in disciplinary referrals, and greater student responsibility as evidenced by assignment completion, grades awarded, and recognized behavior.

The remainder of this chapter pertains to the use of the theory-building processes already discussed, but modified to suit classroom (micro-level) projects. Readers pursuing only school-wide or programwide (macro-level) initiatives may choose to skip ahead to chapter 3.

Leadership Note

The plans communicated by visual theories of action for schoolwide or programwide projects are the heart and soul of what a school and its programs are about. Not only are these implementation roadmaps the result of hours of faculty deliberation, they are a reflection of the best thinking of the collaborative teams that make up the school's faculty. This hard work needs to be recognized, appreciated, and built upon. The more that all stakeholders are familiar with school plans and the rationale behind those plans, the greater the likelihood that the plans will be implemented successfully and consistently. For all these reasons, it is important that administrators and school leaders be conversant with the details of each of the theories of action that have been developed and are being implemented by the PLC teams at their school.

Principals should feel comfortable discussing each schoolwide or programwide visual theory of action and should do so with as much clarity as if they had drafted it themselves. To accomplish this, leaders may wish to:

- Meet with each team individually as it finalizes its visual theories of action.

- Maintain a file and provide copies for all faculty of all the visual theories of action being followed in the school.

- Provide opportunities at faculty meetings for PLC teams to present their visual theories of action.

- Share copies of completed visual theories of action with parents, school district personnel, and accreditation agencies.

A Micro-Level Project

Professional learning communities are dynamic organizations made of committed, passionate educators. As such, it isn't reasonable to expect that all members of a PLC team will always agree on how challenges should be addressed. A functional professional learning community is not a place where everyone holds hands, sings "Kumbaya," and reaches consensus on every issue. In fact, it is unlikely that very much professional learning would occur in a community where everyone was of a single mind. Consensus on methods is nice when it occurs, but it should not be an implicit goal for PLC teamwork.

This lack of urgency about achieving consensus on methods is worth more discussion, as it goes to the heart of a central premise of this book.

Means vs. Ends

There is no question that schools are more effective and students benefit when everyone involved is clear about the school's goals and objectives; these are the *ends* of education. This is why it is so critical that school faculties and PLCs reach consensus on the critical elements of the shared vision, targets, and assessment criteria. While consensus on goals is nearly always beneficial, in many cases requiring educators to employ a particular set of practices—the *means* of education—can actually make schools less effective.

There has been a disturbing trend in education policy in recent years. In many jurisdictions, policymakers and school leaders have mandated expectations for teachers that are grounded more in myth than reality, with the biggest myth being that we already know how to produce universal student success. The professional literature increasingly contains references to proven and/or "research-based" practices, and in many school systems, teachers are required to faithfully implement the district's adopted research-based practices. The clear implication is that there exists an established set of practices that has been shown to succeed with all students in all contexts. Needless to say, if we truly knew what practices would work with all learners, there would be no need for creative educational architecture. Elsewhere, I have referred to the one size fits all strategy as the one-solution syndrome (Sagor, 1995). Over the years, I have repeatedly conducted searches of the literature and have failed to locate a single report of an educational program that has been proven to work with all students. Therefore, the modifier *proven* in the phrase *proven practice* must really mean "proven to work with some students," or perhaps even "many students," but the reality is we have no evidence that any single set of practices works with everyone.

Thus, when teaching colleagues are developing theories of action for implementation in their classrooms, it is perfectly okay for divergent perspectives to emerge, even if they surface within the same PLC team. When this occurs, it should come as no surprise and should be welcomed. Finding that members of a single PLC team, working collaboratively on the same achievement target, hold divergent professional perspectives about how to get there should not derail the project. Rather, recognizing that alternative perspectives exist within the team will open the door for rich professional learning. When teams find they are in disagreement on theories of action, it often leads to a program improvement strategy we will refer to as *alternative pilot projects*.

A main justification for the alternative pilot projects approach is that it provides us with a way to responsibly institute the autonomy component of collective autonomy (Glickman, 1993). In chapter 1, we discussed the importance of having unanimous agreement on shared visions, targets, and assessment criteria. That is the collective aspect of collective autonomy. However, once a team has collectively arrived at shared goals, it is important that it allow maximum autonomy for each educational architect to design innovative strategies to produce universal student success. It should be understood that this approach does not lead to instructional anarchy. When alternative pilot projects are being pursued, every team member's energy and creativity stay focused on a unified purpose: realizing the team-developed *shared* vision. Furthermore, the ultimate success of the alternative pilot projects will be determined by the application of *agreed-upon* assessment criteria.

Classroom-Level Research

Micro-level projects tend to focus on a single student learning attribute rather than on broad program goals such as character development. However, the process for estimating the salience of the independent variables isn't much different than it is for the macro-level project. The significant difference is that when you are working at the classroom (micro) level, you abandon an investment in achieving group consensus.

If you are a member of a grade-level or subject-area PLC team, it is likely that you will be pursuing micro-level action research, because fostering measurable classroom improvement is the primary role of most grade-level or subject-area PLC teams. Frequently, after the adoption of a shared scenario of success or identification of a high-priority program goal, a PLC team will select a specific achievement target for team action. For example, a language arts team might decide to explore how to improve the vocabulary used by students in their writing. When a PLC team convenes to begin this type of work, it is suggested that they determine the salience of the independent variables by following this priority pie process.

1. **Brainstorm individually.** Each member of the team brainstorms on a separate sheet of paper every factor, variable, issue, or phenomena (independent variable) that he or she believes needs attention if this achievement target is to be mastered by every one of the students in his or her classroom. For example, if my team had decided to work on the attribute of vocabulary, I might have brainstormed the following:

    -   Activate prior knowledge.

    -   Use dictionary and thesaurus.

    -   Teach structure of words (prefixes, roots, suffixes).

2. **Proof your list.** Once everyone has generated a personal list of independent variables, the lists are shared. The purpose here isn't to seek consensus, but rather:

    -   To provide everyone with an opportunity to be reminded of anything they may have overlooked

    -   To stimulate fresh thinking and new ideas

    Ultimately, each person's list is considered complete once that person believes it includes all of the key factors, phenomena, or variables he or she needs to attend to so all students can achieve proficiency on the target.

3. **Assess the salience of the independent variables.** Using the same Independent Variable Assessment Form that was used with the macro projects (page 50), each member lists the independent variables in his or her list. Once all the variables are listed, ask,

"How important is this factor, phenomena, or variable to my students' ultimate success on this achievement target?" Based upon how they answer that question, members assign a percentage to that item based on their assessment of its relative importance to the achievement of universal success on this target. The total of the awarded percentages must add up to one hundred.

Finally, on the bottom of the Independent Variable Assessment Form, a pie graph should be drawn displaying the percentages assigned to each independent variable. The pie charts become a reflection of each member's perspective on what will need to be done to produce universal success on this target. Figure 2.4 is a priority pie I prepared for assisting my students in developing proficiency with vocabulary.

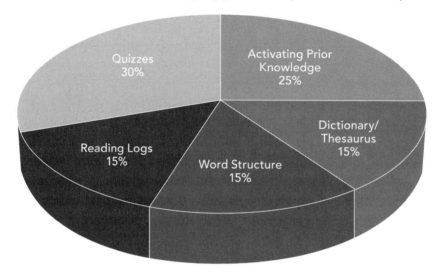

Figure 2.4: Priority pie for building vocabulary.

If it turns out that a number of the members perceive the salience of the key independent variables in a similar way, that is fine. This means that multiple team members share the same theoretical perspective, a nice outcome. If, however, distinctly different theories of action emerge, it portends valuable professional learning for the team. Nothing is more helpful for teasing out what actually makes a difference for students than comparing and contrasting alternative approaches to achieving success on the same target.

Once each of the PLC team members have developed priority pies, each member writes a summary statement explaining his or her emerging theory. Here is the summary statement I wrote to explain my emerging theory on vocabulary instruction, as illustrated in my priority pie (fig 2.4):

> I believe there are five factors I need to attend to if my students are to become proficient at developing their vocabularies. The most critical is study and practice (30 percent), and this will be accomplished through quizzes and assignments. The next most powerful factor (25 percent) is the activation of prior knowledge. The three other factors, which are equal in importance, are my instruction on how to use reference materials (15 percent), direct instruction and practice with word

structure (15 percent), and students pulling words from their reading and capturing these in their reading logs (15 percent).

In circumstances when multiple pies emerged from a single PLC team, copies of each pie, along with the summary narrative statements, should be distributed to every member of the team. At this stage, the team can proudly report:

> We have met and considered what it might take to help all of our students achieve proficiency on this target. A number of promising alternative perspectives emerged. Over the next few months, we will be implementing a variety of alternative instructional strategies in our classrooms and assessing their effectiveness based on common assessment criteria. Once the assessments are complete, the team will convene to discuss the results obtained and make future plans.

Leadership Note

If teachers believe they are under pressure to reach consensus, they will do so, and expeditiously. No one likes to waste time in meetings. Consequently, when a faculty feels they must agree before adjourning, there is often undue pressure to achieve agreement quickly without adequately thinking through the ramifications.

For this reason, the more the faculty believes leadership is genuinely excited about the potential professional learning that comes from comparing and contrasting alternative perspectives, the more likely they will be to engage in rigorous thinking, debate, and planning.

Leadership can foster this belief by:

- Applauding teams when alternative perspectives have been explored

- Inviting teams to share their alternative perspectives at faculty meetings and curriculum nights

- Scheduling opportunities for PLC teams to report to colleagues on what they've learned or are learning in panel presentations that feature alternative perspectives

Building the Visual Theory of Action

When we are speaking of a graphic reconstruction at the micro level, we are generally talking about a depiction of the specific actions that will occur inside an individual teacher's classroom. For this reason, a visual theory of action for a classroom (micro-level) intervention might be thought of as a visual lesson plan. Earlier, when discussing macro-level projects, it was stated that each professional who will play a role in implementing an action should participate in the development of the theory that informs those actions. When departmental or grade-level PLC teams create visual theories of action, a separate graphic should be produced for each unique priority pie. In some circumstances, this could mean that every member of the PLC team will be drawing his or her own visual theory of action, or alternatively, several people may choose to collaborate on a single one. If a team member holds a particular perspective on how a target should be addressed, it's crucial that person participate in fleshing out a visual theory of action consistent with his or her perspective.

Figure 2.5 (page 47) is an example of a visual theory of action prepared by a hypothetical teacher. It depicts her strategy for developing student responsibility through the use of democratic class meetings.

Similar to the visual theory of action employed at the macro level, classroom-based implementation roadmaps should specify the actions to be taken, the barriers to be overcome, and the interventions that must occur to create the conditions for universal student success. The following set of nine steps will guide you through the preparation of a visual theory of action for use with classroom-level projects.

1. **Assemble the necessary materials.** Each person or group of colleagues needs a large sheet of poster paper that can be laid across a table or posted on a wall. They will also need pads of different-colored sticky notes and a supply of felt-tip pens.

2. **Clarify the shared vision or target.** Individually or as a group, take a moment to review what universal student success will look like on the target that is to be the focus of this initiative. You may wish to review the team's shared vision pertaining to this learner outcome.

3. **Brainstorm individually.** Using the Visual Theory of Action Planning Form (page 51), individually brainstorm all the actions, factors, and phenomena that you (and those working with you) believe will affect success in hitting this target.

4. **Share the lists.** There may be other members of your team who are approaching this target in a fundamentally different way and, consequently, preparing their own visual theories of action. As your immediate colleagues, friends, and peers, your teammates will be an excellent resource to help you identify factors that may have been left off your list.

5. **Orient the graphic.** On the extreme right side, indicate the desired outcome. This is where you will end up when all your students have met your target and you have fully realized the shared vision. On the extreme left, the current situation, place any data you have on current performance.

6. **Drawing the theory of action.** On separate sticky notes, write out each action, factor, or phenomena that remains on the list you generated. Now, arrange these sticky notes on your poster paper in a manner that will display a clear process, which your students can move from their current condition to the desired outcome.

7. **Proof the graphic.** Once you feel your visual theory of action is complete, make a list of the different types of students in your class, such as:

    - Boys
    - High performers
    - Girls
    - Low performers

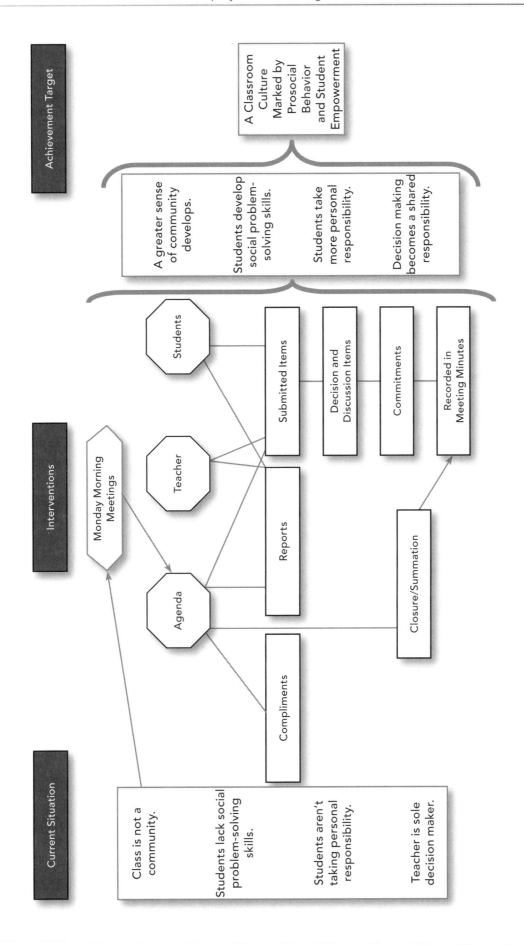

Figure 2.5: Visual theory of action of a strategy to implement democratic class meetings.

Now mentally walk through your graphic in the shoes of each of these categories of students. As you take your walk, look for places where this type of student might get derailed. If you encounter such a roadblock, consider how you might design a way around that obstacle, and add your workaround to the visual theory of action. Your theory is now ready to be shared.

8. **Solicit feedback.** Once you have finished proofing your visual theory of action, it is a good idea to have a set of critical friends review it. If you are a member of a PLC team, you already have the perfect group of professional colleagues to be your critical friends group—your teammates. Begin by briefly explaining your plan to the other members. Then ask them to respond to question 1 on the Visual Theory of Action Feedback Form (page 52): "In 150 words or less, explain what is being proposed." Then have your teammates share what they've written. If they captured the essence of what you are proposing, you will know your graphic is communicating effectively. To the degree that their responses vary from what you had intended, it means you will need to make revisions to your graphic. Finally, ask your colleagues if there is anything you should add to the theory of action to make success more likely and to communicate your intentions more clearly.

9. **Consider the feedback and revise the graphic.** Reflect on the feedback from your critical friends, and adjust your visual theory of action accordingly. Now, write a brief narrative description of the actions and interactions depicted on your graphic reconstruction. What follows is a narrative description written to accompany the visual theory on class meetings shown in figure 2.5 (page 47).

> I am implementing weekly democratic class meetings in an effort to create a classroom culture that fosters prosocial behavior and student empowerment. This is vitally important, since many of my students currently lack effective social skills and avoid taking personal responsibility for their actions. My classroom has become a place where the teacher is the sole decision maker, and there is no sense of community.
>
> Among the barriers I will be facing are the prevailing student expectations and attitudes. Students feel powerless and have become comfortable with their passive role. When things don't go as the students would like, they seem to take solace by blaming someone else.
>
> I will chair the weekly class meetings and follow an agenda with four parts: (1) open compliment time, (2) reports on previous business, (3) new items submitted by me or the students, and (4) closure. Most matters of classroom policy will be dealt with as decision items; however, if the issue concerns a school policy about which a final decision is not in our hands, the issue will be handled as a discussion item. I will follow up on all discussion items and report back to the classroom community. At the conclusion of each discussion or decision item, the members of the classroom community will make commitments to each other. These commitments will be recorded in the meeting minutes. I will make liberal use of student subcommittees to ensure a hundred percent student participation.

I expect that the weekly class meetings and follow up sessions will result in more shared decision making, a greater sense of classroom community, improved social problem-solving skills, and students taking more personal responsibility for their actions.

Leadership Note

Just as it was important that leadership understand the theories of action that govern the teaching and the programs operating in their schools, it is imperative that all the members of a PLC team are cognizant of how their teammates carry out instruction, particularly instruction that is aimed at achieving the team's shared vision. This can only happen through dialogue aimed at deprivatizing teaching.

One way to encourage teachers to participate in this kind of dialogue is for leadership to find frequent opportunities to ask teachers about the theories of action they are implementing, as well as asking them to reflect on how their approach may differ from approaches used by other members of their PLC team. As teachers become accustomed to safely and openly discussing their theories of action and comparing and contrasting their personal approaches with others, they will become more comfortable asking about and learning from what their colleagues are doing.

Conclusion

The essence of Habit of Inquiry 2, Articulating Theories of Action, is to create a plan that will be able to guide you on your journey into unfamiliar territory. A well-articulated visual theory of action provides a comprehensive, thoughtful outline of a set of professional actions designed to produce universal student success with a valued outcome, and it does so with *face validity*. Having face validity means any reasonable person (lay person or professional) who takes the time to review a theory of action would predict that it has a high likelihood of getting the students to the desired outcome.

Once the members of a PLC team have developed comprehensive theories of action and shared their theories with stakeholders, they have completed the most arduous aspect of the entire collaborative action research process. More importantly, by developing a thoughtful and clearly articulated theory of action, you are ready to commence work on your project with the confidence that you are following a path with a high likelihood of success.

Independent Variable Assessment Form

Target:

List all factors, variables, phenomena, and categories of actions that will be necessary for all students to achieve success on this achievement target.

Item	Percentage

Construct your priority pie in the space below:

Visual Theory of Action Planning Form

Target:

List all the **actions** required to achieve universal success with this target:

List all the **factors** (demographics, personality, history, and so on) that must be taken into account to realize universal success with this target:

List all the **phenomena** (student prerequisites, nature of content to be studied, and so on) that will need to be taken into account to realize universal success with this target:

List all the **barriers** that may be encountered as we attempt to realize success for all students on this target:

List **anything else** that you feel is relevant to realizing universal success with this target:

Visual Theory of Action Feedback Form

This form is to be used by critical friends to provide feedback to the creator(s) of a visual theory of action. Before answering the following questions, carefully review the visual theory of action and any narrative material that was developed to accompany it.

Target:

1.   In 150 words or less, explain what is being proposed.

2.   Is there anything that should be added to the graphic to make it more likely to succeed?

Habit of Inquiry
Acting Purposefully
While Collecting Data

Thus far you have dealt with two Habits of Inquiry: Clarifying a Shared Vision for Success and Articulating Theories of Action. This was important work, and hopefully, these exercises helped you reflect on your values and your best thinking. But it has yet to be determined if the values and ideas reflected in your shared vision and the actions enunciated in your visual theory of action will succeed in getting your students to the desired outcome of universal student success. This is why Habit of Inquiry 3, Acting Purposefully While Collecting Data, is so critical. Understanding the real-world effectiveness of your theory of action will be essential if your collaborative action research is to produce the professional learning sought by you and your colleagues.

The Three Impact Questions

It is often said that one of the most difficult aspects of the action research process is finding a research question worth investigating. Furthermore, it has been suggested that the first step of the inquiry process be the development of research questions. Although this makes sense when the action research project is being conducted by and for an individual practitioner, the purpose and function of the research question is quite different when the research is being conducted as part of PLC work.

If you are a member of a PLC team, you are approaching your action research already aware that the purpose of your PLC is to collaboratively discover ways to foster universal student success on priority achievement targets. Therefore, your essential action research question was set when your team chose a target for the team to pursue. That question was, "What will it take to produce universal student success with _____?"

Still, if you are to succeed in producing the professional knowledge and developing the insight you are after, three subquestions will need to become a routine part of your inquiry.

These key subquestions for PLC action research are called *impact questions*, as their focus is the impact of the instructional initiative and the professional actions that influenced that impact. Taken together, the answers to the three impact questions will assist you in understanding what worked, for which students they worked, and why. Each impact question is designed to help you explore one of three phenomena: action, change, and relationship. The three impact questions are:

1. "What specifically did I (we) do?" (action)

2. "What improvement occurred for my (our) students?" (change)

3. "What was the relationship between my (our) actions and changes in performance?" (relationship)

Answering the Impact Questions

Answering these questions involves the collection of data. The busy educator is often averse to this, because it implies stealing time from instruction. There are two reasons that you need not be overly concerned about the time demands of data collection. First, the data that you will need are close at hand. Second, much of the data you will want to use for your action research is already being collected for other purposes (such as assessments, grades, and student portfolios). Today's schools and classrooms are already data-rich environments. In this chapter, we will explore twelve sample strategies that will enable your PLC team to use readily available data to efficiently and effectively answer the three impact questions. These strategies involve the use of both qualitative and quantitative research methods, as well as formative and summative assessment techniques.

Qualitative vs. Quantitative Research

In the most basic sense, *quantitative research* refers to the collection of information that is numerical in nature. Quantitative research methods are usually used to report on phenomena that can be objectively measured. Quantitative data—specifically data obtained through standardized testing—are routinely used to report on the effectiveness of school programs.

Creswell (2009, p. 4) defines qualitative research as "a means for exploring and understanding the meaning individuals or groups ascribe to a social or human problem." Qualitative data are obtained through such devices as observations, interviews, surveys, and analyses of artifacts such as lesson plans and student work.

For our purposes, the key difference between these two categories of research pertains to the question being asked and answered. Quantitative data will be utilized, although not exclusively, to help you build a response to Impact Question 1, "What specifically did I (we) do?" and Impact Question 2, "What improvement occurred for my (our) students?" However, if you relied only on quantitative data to answer those questions, you would likely be unsatisfied, because numbers alone can't provide the professional learning you are seeking. By strategically adding some qualitative data, you will be able to gain insights into why and how things occurred as they did.

For example, when pursuing an answer to Impact Question 1, "What specifically did I (we) do?" you will likely want to report on the amount of time (quantitative data) spent on certain instructional activities. But just knowing *how* your time was spent won't tell you much. You will want to dig deeper into your instructional decision making. For example, you may wish to know, "Why did I end up spending more time on cooperative learning than teacher-directed instruction?" Likewise when exploring Impact Question 2, "What improvement occurred for my (our) students?" you might want to know more than just the amount of learning that occurred. You may also be interested in finding out, "Why did more learning occur for some students than others?" To answer questions such as these, you will need to employ qualitative methods.

Likewise, to satisfactorily answer Impact Question 3, "What was the relationship between my (our) actions and changes in performance?" you will find that a combination of quantitative and qualitative data provides the best results. The twelve strategies explored in this chapter provide examples of both quantitative and qualitative methods.

Summative vs. Formative Assessments

To answer the three impact questions, you will also need to use both summative and formative assessment. Summative assessment generally comes at the end of instruction and is used to determine and certify what students have learned. Assessment expert Rick Stiggins (2001) explains that summative assessment provides evidence of student competence or program effectiveness and informs us about what must come next. He points out that while there is much value in summative assessment, it is of little motivational value for students or teachers.

Formative assessment, on the other hand, occurs during instruction and is used to make midcourse corrections in our teaching. Stiggins (2001) defines formative assessments as both formal and informal processes that teachers and students use to gather evidence in order to improve learning. For teachers, formative assessment provides timely feedback on the influence their actions are having on their students, and for students, it provides direction and motivation.

In many schools, significant amounts of quantitative data (at least pertaining to standards) are already being collected and analyzed. The quantitative data most schools have available come from the summative assessments produced by the standardized instruments mandated and conducted by the state and/or district. For this reason, most teachers already possess significant information on how well their students have been performing on quantitative standardized measures. Not infrequently, grade-level and departmental PLC teams are charged with effecting a positive change in those scores. Unfortunately, the reports about student performance from standardized tests usually don't arrive at the school building until after instruction has concluded. Therefore, they provide little benefit to the teacher who is seeking insight on how to adjust instruction for a particular group of students. DuFour, DuFour, and Eaker (2008) commented that this creates the DRIP syndrome (schools that are data rich but information poor). Teachers suffering from the DRIP syndrome have lots of data, but lack the information needed to improve instruction. Another problem with an over-reliance on summative assessment is that these data focus exclusively on the outcomes of teaching while providing little or no insight into the teaching process itself.

This is why PLC teams often find the qualitative formative data that can be routinely collected during instruction to be extremely beneficial. As instructors, we desire information on what is motivating a student and what strategies are working or not working, as well as how a particular student feels about instruction. This is the type of information and data that can shed light on the dynamics of the teaching and learning process and provide the foundation for the professional learning that PLC teams are seeking.

The approach followed in this text is called *mixed methods research* (Creswell, 2009; Tashakkori & Teddlie, 2003). This paradigm recognizes that meaningful professional learning requires an integration of qualitative and quantitative, statistical and attitudinal, data. Mixed methods research also recognizes that creative professional educators have motivational and informational needs that can be satisfied only through a combination of summative and formative data.

The Function of the Three Impact Questions

We will continue our exploration of Habit of Inquiry 3, Acting Purposefully While Collecting Data, by exploring in some detail the function of each of the three impact questions.

Impact Question 1: "What Specifically Did I (We) Do?"

Science moves forward by scientists' publishing their findings and others attempting to replicate the results. When subsequent trials reach similar conclusions, the validity of the initial findings is reinforced. For this process to be effective, each scientific report must contain a detailed explanation of the processes utilized as well as the interventions attempted. Other scholars cannot evaluate reported findings and advance the knowledge base unless they know the experimental methodology used; they need to understand precisely what the original investigators did and how their inquiry was conducted.

Of course, your primary goal may not be the advancement of the science of teaching and learning. You are probably more interested in determining the effectiveness of your theory of action with your particular students. However, if it turns out that your theory of action worked to perfection—every one of your students mastered the content, and everyone did a perfect job of hitting all the achievement targets—then you will definitely want to repeat your success the next time you teach this material. It could, however, prove difficult to replicate your own earlier results unless you can recall precisely what actions you and your students took that resulted in things working out as well as they did.

Frequently, due to the rushed nature of school life, we set goals, assess our students on what they learned, and then wring our hands or celebrate based on the results obtained. Unfortunately, there is often a big black hole between our goal setting and the data on student performance. If, however, we are in possession of good data on exactly what transpired for both students and teachers, we can remove some of the mystery from that black hole.

Leadership Note

While Impact Question 1, "What specifically did I (we) do?" is the most straightforward, it can be hard for many PLC teams to address. The norms of many schools, grade levels, and departments are such that the actions taken by individual teachers in the privacy of their own classrooms are considered private business. While educators have become comfortable discussing student performance, they are far less comfortable sharing information on their own instructional decision making.

This is why nearly every advocate for professional learning communities has argued for the deprivatization of teaching. One good way to accomplish this is through modeling. School leaders can be a source of this modeling by conducting action research, focused on their own leadership, and by doing so transparently. The public act of collecting and reporting data on what the school leadership is doing and what choices leadership is making will make the deprivatization of teaching more likely to occur.

Impact Question 2: "What Improvement Occurred for My (Our) Students?"

For committed professional educators, the only justification for investing time and energy in PLC work is to stimulate significant gains in student performance. Habit of Inquiry 1, Clarifying a Shared Vision for Success, introduced you to a visioning process designed to help teams clearly articulate the attributes they hoped to see developed as a consequence of their instruction. It was suggested that teams reflect on these attributes (achievement targets) through the creation of behavioral rating scales (rubrics). You will now be able to use the rubrics you developed when working on Habit of Inquiry 1 to help you document both individual and group progress on your targets.

Many PLC teams routinely discuss student performance data. Unfortunately, too often those discussions generally occur *after* instruction has been completed. Furthermore, the data reflect only what the students knew or were able to do at the end of the instructional period. Detailed information on how the students learned and progressed to that point is often lacking. For example, did growth occur at a consistent rate throughout the instructional period? Did certain activities stimulate more growth than others? Did every student grow at an equal rate? These and many other questions cannot be answered satisfactorily by any single end-of-term or standardized assessment. When, however, we are able to take the pulse of each student on a regular basis and use those readings to monitor their response to each of our instructional interventions, we are able to gain a perspective on which teacher actions correlated with which increases in student performance, and which actions didn't correspond to changes in performance.

Impact Question 3: "What Was the Relationship Between My (Our) Actions and Changes in Performance?"

Uncovering a correlation between a set of teacher actions and positive changes in student performance doesn't necessarily mean that the identified actions "caused" the changes observed. While proving causation in social science is never entirely possible, we can take steps that will provide us with more confidence in the relationship between our interventions and the results obtained. At the same time, we must be careful not to take credit for improvement that was, in reality, due to factors other than our teaching. Conversely, unless we take care, we can find ourselves feeling guilty over negative outcomes that were outside of our control.

To illustrate this phenomena, I'll use the example of a community I lived in, a lovely town with a long, proud history. Not very long ago, it was a semirural mill town located twenty miles from a major metropolitan area. In recent years, the mill has significantly cut production and made corresponding cuts to its workforce. Simultaneously, a shortage of housing in the metropolitan area resulted in the rapid development of the rural local real estate into high-end residential housing with lovely mountain and river views. Consequently, this community is no longer a blue-collar, working-class town. Now, the majority of homeowners are highly educated professionals who work in the nearby city.

During this period of transition, student test scores in the local schools have steadily risen. This doesn't surprise me, as these schools are very good, and the teachers are extremely dedicated. However, if we were to assert that the only explanation for the sharp rise in test scores was the quality of the teaching, we would be discounting the dramatic change in the student body and the influence that family aspirations and economic advantage exert on student performance.

Another example comes from a middle school in Texas, where I worked with a PLC team that had decided to implement a highly regarded schoolwide program designed to improve school climate and encourage prosocial student behavior. This middle school served a community largely made up of military families attached to the local army base. The teachers did a magnificent job of implementing their climate improvement program; when the year ended, however, the data suggested that student behavior had actually deteriorated. Did this mean the teachers implemented the program incorrectly? Did it mean the program was not as good as its developers contended? Those were both plausible explanations. But consider one additional fact: during this period, the U.S. military was engaged in two overseas combat missions. The majority of the students at this school had at least one parent who had been deployed to a combat zone or was on notice that he or she might be deployed in the immediate future. Given the emotional turmoil in the lives of these students, it was only logical to expect those out-of-school factors to have some influence on school and classroom behavior.

The point of these examples is that students may, on occasion, demonstrate improvement or even regress for reasons outside of our control. Therefore, it is important that we use data collection strategies that will enable us to fully examine the relationship between actions and outcomes.

We will now look at twelve specific data collection strategies that have worked effectively for both individual action researchers and PLC team action research. Our discussion will be organized around the three impact questions.

Data Collection Strategies

There are numerous ways to collect data to answer the three impact questions. As you develop your action research data collection plan, it is a good idea to organize your thoughts using the Data Collection Planning Matrix (page 81). It is strongly suggested that you use multiple sources of data to answer each impact question. To ensure greater validity and reliability, action researchers generally use multiple independent sources of data, a method known as *triangulation*. Build your triangulated data collection plan one impact question at a time. The best way to do this is to read through the sample data collection strategies for each of the impact questions, and then decide which of those techniques are a good fit for your project. It isn't essential that you use the strategies suggested in this chapter. Action researchers can use a vast number of techniques and instruments to acquire the data they need. It is, however, essential that, before proceeding any further, you produce a triangulated data collection plan that will enable you to confidently answer each of the three impact questions.

Another suggestion: don't be intimidated by the number of steps you see delineated for a particular strategy. Many of these steps will be completed in just a few minutes or less. Each of these approaches can easily be implemented by a busy educator. The reason for providing such detailed instructions is to make the use of these techniques as clear as possible. Nevertheless, you are encouraged to develop a data collection plan that makes sense for you in light of your assignment and your other time demands.

Data Collection Strategies for Impact Question 1: "What Specifically Did I (We) Do?"

Most teachers find collecting the data to answer this question the least taxing aspect of the entire action research process. All that is required is documentation of the instructional actions taken and the time invested in helping students achieve success with a particular academic goal or achievement target. While this is straightforward and shouldn't prove overly time consuming, it shouldn't be left to the last minute. If I were to try to reconstruct everything I did with my students at the end of a forty-five-day, nine-week quarter, my recollections would prove to be anything but sharp. However, if I engage in a few additional steps designed to structure the recollection process, my documentation regarding my instructional actions will prove quite accurate.

Time Use Charting

Review your visual theory of action as developed in the last chapter. This review should bring back to the surface each of the actions that you deemed essential for your students to succeed with your chosen achievement target. Then follow these eight simple steps.

1. Using the Pre-Intervention Time Expectation Worksheet (page 82), list the key actions or events you and the students will be expected to be engaged with, and make a guess at the average number of minutes (per week) of classroom time that you will be devoting to each of these actions. Should an activity occur on just one or two occasions throughout the term, list the total number of minutes that will be devoted to the activity in column three, and note this in the comments column.

2. Look at your list and ask yourself, "Is there anything else that I plan on doing that is essential to helping my students achieve success on this target that is not represented on this list?" If you come up with any, add those items to the list, and adjust the time allocations accordingly.

3. Now, total up the class time you anticipate spending in pursuit of this target (the total number of minutes in column three), and divide that number by the number of weeks in the term. The figure represents the average number of minutes (weekly) you anticipate investing in this project over the course of this study. To determine the percentage of time anticipated for each category of action, divide the total classtime by the total minutes to be spent on the project. The answer should be noted as a percentage and then placed in the last column. Figure 3.1 is an example of a filled-out Pre-Intervention Time Expectation Worksheet.

Actions (From Visual Theory of Action)	Approximate Class Time to Be Invested (in Minutes Per Week)	Total Class Time to Be Invested During the Term	Comment	Percentage of Time to Be Invested
Jigsaw Activities	45	405		26%
Class Discussions	30	270		17%
Individual Work Time	40	360		24%
Quizzes/Tests	20	180	Ten-minute quizzes on Fridays and 3 half-hour tests	12%
Pair Sharing	15	135		9%
Presentations	20	180	Presentations will occur 3 times for approximately 1 hour each time	12%
Total	170	1,530		100%

Figure 3.1: Sample pre-intervention time expectation worksheet for fifth-grade social studies.

4. Once you have a percentage for each anticipated category of action (column five), draw a pie graph illustrating how you anticipate spending your instructional time. This is your pre-intervention time expectation pie chart. You may find that this graph closely resembles the priority pie you prepared in the last chapter, but it serves a different purpose. The pie chart you have just produced is your best guess at what will be required in terms of your time and professional action to achieve universal success for your students with this target. Figure 3.2 is an example of a pie chart made from the data in figure 3.1 (page 60).

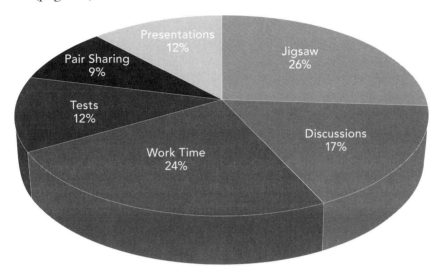

Figure 3.2: Pie chart for pre-intervention time expectations.

When using time use charting as part of your data collection plan, it is essential that your lesson plan book contain an accurate record of what you did in class during the study period. My lesson plan book rarely provided me with accurate documentation of the work the students and I did in class. This wasn't because I am a bad planner, rather it was because I frequently changed plans on the spot based on student needs and circumstances. I think that is just good teaching. However, it resulted in a lesson plan book that was something less than a valid reflection of what transpired in class. This is easily remedied, and your plan book can be transformed into a valuable source of data if you add one small task to your weekly routine. On Friday afternoon, after the students leave the room, simply sit down with the past week's lesson plans and adjust them to reflect the reality of what transpired in your class that week.

5. Make a copy of the Weekly Time Use Worksheet (page 83). In the left-hand column, list all the categories of action that became slices of pie on your pre-intervention pie chart. Once the categories of action have been added to the worksheet, make copies so you have one per week for the duration of your study. Keep these copies in your lesson plan book.

6. Every Friday afternoon, after you finish updating your lesson plans to reflect what actually occurred, take out your Weekly Time Use Worksheet, and indicate your recollection of the number of minutes, if any, spent that week for each listed action. Adding

your thoughts regarding the nature of the work in the comment column may prove helpful later when you are doing data analysis.

7. At the end of the term (or the conclusion of the study), calculate the total time spent on the project and subtotals for each category. Then, calculate the percentage of time spent on each category of instructional activity, and enter it in the right-hand column.

Figure 3.3 (page 63) is an example of a completed Weekly Time Use Worksheet.

8. The final step (which cannot be completed until you've finished your intervention) is the preparation of a second pie graph, one illustrating the actual use of class time during the course of the project.

By placing the pre-intervention expected time use graph and the actual time usage graph side by side (fig. 3.4, page 64), you will be able to quickly see whether the time actually spent was consistent with what you had anticipated or if things played out differently than you had initially planned.

Weekly Time Summaries

This strategy documents what occurred with an individual learner over a period of time, using records that can be kept by the student. This can be accomplished in a number of ways. One approach is to require students to fill out a 3" × 5" index card similar to the one illustrated in figure 3.5 (page 65) at the end of instruction each day. All you need to provide the students is the total amount of time allocated for this subject that day. Then, on Friday, ask them to use these cards to total up how their time was spent during the past week using the Student Weekly Time Log (page 84).

You can easily collect additional qualitative data from students as they fill out their Student Weekly Time Log. For example, I might add one or more of the following additional questions to this form:

- Please rate on a scale of 1 to 10 how hard you worked this week, with 10 meaning as hard as possible and 1 meaning you didn't put forth any effort.

- Please rate how successful you were this week on a scale of 1 to 10, with 10 meaning you did excellent work and 1 meaning your work was quite poor.

- What did you enjoy most about our class this week? (Be as specific as possible.)

- What will you do differently next week?

The simple act of filling out these forms and collating their own responses provides students with valuable insights into their personal choices. In the example shown in figure 3.6 (page 66), Sarah can see that this particular week she spent considerably more time (40 minutes) listening to her group than she spent actively discussing (0 minutes).

Category of Action	Week 1	Week 2	Week 3	Week 4	Week 5	Week 6	Week 7	Week 8	Week 9	Totals	Percentage of Time Use
Cooperative Learning	75	60	60	15	60	75	20	20	20	405	12%
Projects	0	0	90	150	150	90	150	150	75	855	27%
Guest Speakers/ Media	60	90	90	15	30	90	120	120	0	615	19%
Discussions	150	100	45	30	30	30	0	15	120	520	16%
Lecture	20	20	20	30	30	45	20	15	15	215	7%
Review	30	30	60	60	60	60	60	60	125	545	17%
Totals:	335	300	365	300	360	390	370	380	355	3155	98%

Figure 3.3: Completed weekly time use worksheet.

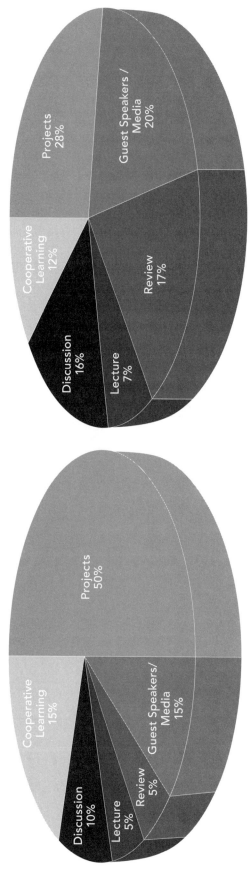

Figure 3.4: Pie graphs comparing pre-intervention expectations to actual time usage.

Name: _____   Today's Date: _____   Length of Class: _____

List the things you did during today's class and how much time you spent doing each thing on your list:

_____

_____

_____

_____

_____

_____

_____

_____

_____

_____

_____

_____

Figure 3.5: Sample index card for student-kept records.

Finally, at the end of the term, you may wish to ask your students to use a Student Weekly Time Log (page 84) to produce a composite report of their work during the term. Having your students become active participants in documenting their own learning inevitably leads to their taking more responsibility for their actions and the consequences of those.

Shadowing

So far, we have looked at strategies for using your records and student self-reports to describe the actions occurring in class. Another strategy that provides significant insight into what is transpiring in the classroom is shadowing. Shadowing is the process of following or walking behind someone in order to see things through their eyes. Because it would be impractical to shadow all of our students or to shadow any one student for an extended period of time, when conducting shadowing as part of PLC team action research, we will generally observe a sample of students and do so for just a few instructional periods. Members of a PLC team often assist each other in this effort by volunteering to shadow students attending class in a colleague's classroom. The process works as follows.

1. **The teacher selects a sample of students to be shadowed (no more than three).**
    I suggest picking students for shadowing who are representative of the class as a whole. For example, I might select one student who is among my highest achievers, one who is a middle achiever, and one who is a low performer. Other times, teachers will select the students whom they are most concerned about for shadowing.

Student Weekly Time Log

Name: *Sarah*

Class: _____

Activity	Monday	Tuesday	Wednesday	Thursday	Friday
Worksheets	5 min.		5 min.		5 min.
Pair Share	5 min.		5 min.	5 min.	
Listening to Group	10 min.		10 min.	5 min.	15 min.
Teaching My Group					5 min.
Listening to Teacher		10 min.		10 min.	
Discussing With My Group					
Reading					5 min.
Talking					
Off-Task		10 min.			
Total Time:	20 min.	20 min.	20 min.	20 min.	30 min.

Please circle the number that indicates how hard you worked this week:

1   2   3   4   5   6   7   8   9   10

No Effort ⟵——————————————————⟶ Very Hard

Figure 3.6: Sarah's weekly time log.

2. **Determine what you want to know about the students' classroom experience.** Are you interested in measures of engagement (on-task behavior, intensity of effort, or active versus passive participation), cognitive level of their work, choices they are making, or something else? Then consider how this action or behavior might be observed by a colleague visiting your room.

3. **The shadowing occurs.** I suggest that rather than shadowing each individual student, the shadower position him- or herself to observe all three of the shadowed students simultaneously and inconspicuously. This way the identified students will not need to

know (at this point) that they are the focus of the data collection, and consequently, they will behave in their normal fashion. While shadowing, the shadower collects the agreed-upon observational data (step 2) pertaining to the identified students.

4. **Conduct a perception check**. Once the shadowing period has been completed (usually one or two teaching episodes), the person doing the shadowing conducts a perception check with each of the observed students. This is done by approaching each student individually and privately asking, "As you know, I have been observing in your class for the past few days. During this time, I have particularly noticed you and your actions in class. I wondered if it would be okay for me to ask you a few questions about your work?"

    If the student says yes (I find that they always do), then the observer shares his perceptions and asks if the student agrees with those observations. If the student disagrees, the shadower asks the student why. Keep in mind that one's focus as a shadower is to document observable actions or behavior, not to make inferences regarding any particular student's motivation.

5. **Report results.** The teacher conducting the shadowing reports his or her observations, along with the student perceptions of those observations, to the classroom teacher.

Shadowing is a wonderful window into the world of the students. At West Linn High School in Oregon, where I served as principal, each year the faculty would select schoolwide issues to investigate collaboratively. One of the data collection techniques we routinely used was the shadowing of students, followed by a report to the faculty (Sagor, 1981). Because we were interested in understanding the students' total school experience, we shadowed students for an entire day. For us, this would require twelve days of substitute teachers as we followed three students at each of the four grade levels. We secured permission first from the students (whose names had been drawn to produce a stratified random sample), and the shadowing occurred on consecutive days to avoid the disrupting influence of too many substitutes in the building on any single day.

At the end of the shadowing experience, the twelve participating teachers and twelve students reported at a faculty meeting on what we called "A Day in the Life." Our annual shadowing was one of the most significant factors in deprivatizing teaching at our school. In addition, it opened up a powerful dialogue with the student body about the student experience. This activity became so popular and so many teachers volunteered to participate that we had to select shadowers by drawing names from a hat. Not only did we learn a great deal about our school, but teachers consistently reported that it was the best professional development they had ever received. Consider this: by spending a day shadowing during "A Day in the Life," these teachers were able to visit seven different colleagues' classrooms, and the only cost for all this collegial learning was the cost of one substitute teacher.

Leadership Note

Many teachers become uncomfortable when asked to publicly discuss the information documented in response to Impact Question 1, for numerous reasons. Some teachers feel discussing their instruction is akin to bragging or violates the cultural norm that what happens inside the four walls of a classroom should be kept inside those same four walls. Other teachers have developed a fear that if they are too open about the instructional challenges they are encountering, they may be risking their job security. These are logical fears.

It is important that leadership be seen as welcoming open discussion of classroom environments and instructional strategies. To accomplish this, leadership needs to avoid being seen as having anointed certain practices above all others. When teachers think that the school leadership believes there is just one accepted way to teach, those who operate differently will often clam up, fearing they will be labeled as an outcast or an obstructionist. The reality is that everyone teaches somewhat differently, and it is good to allow one's personality to emerge in the classroom. Often, it is these unique instructional decisions that make the biggest difference in student learning.

If, however, we don't openly explore the differences between what students experience in different programs and different classrooms, we will lose the opportunity to sort out and understand what it is that really matters and truly influences student learning.

Leadership can model deprivatization by engaging in the act of teaching alongside regular classroom teachers and openly sharing what teachers and their students are learning and doing. During my ten years as a building administrator, I always assigned myself one regular class to teach. While this proved time consuming, I found it paid huge dividends. As the teachers saw their principal struggling with the same issues they were facing, they became much more comfortable with an open, honest dialogue on the challenges of teaching and learning.

In addition, leadership should encourage and facilitate teachers visiting each other's rooms to see the unique ways students are being taught in the same school or program. Finally, leadership can structure opportunities both at PLC team meetings and faculty meetings for a discussion of the dynamics of individual classroom and teaching decisions.

Data Collection Strategies for Impact Question 2: "What Improvement Occurred for My (Our) Students?"

The purpose of the data you collected in response to Impact Question 2 is to help you understand any changes in student performance that occurred during the course of your study. One-shot summative assessments tell us if growth occurred, but they do so without referencing what stimulated that growth. As was pointed out earlier, these assessments usually occur so late in the process that it is impossible for the teacher to make any necessary adjustments. Therefore, as an action researcher, you will find it important to use formative assessment as part of your data collection plan. Specifically, you will want to use numerous sensitive, incremental measures of student development. The following data collection strategies should help you elicit this information.

Rating Scales

In your work on Habit of Inquiry 1, in which you articulated your shared vision, you created a behavioral rating scale that contained criteria for use in measuring success on your priority achievement targets (page 22). Those rating scales can now be used as data collection instruments as you assemble data in response to Impact Question 2, "What improvement occurred for my (our) students?" In fact, a behavioral rating scale is a single instrument that can provide you with two independent sources of data: your professional assessment of student learning and the student's self-assessment of his or her own learning.

If you elect to use this strategy, you (and the student) should use the rating scale to assess performance prior to beginning your intervention. Later, after instruction has concluded, you can conduct a post-assessment and compare the two scores to document the degree of growth that was observed over time. Later, you may choose to further aggregate these scores by gender, poverty status, prior achievement level, or any other demographic factors you may deem relevant. The aggregation and disaggregation process will be discussed at greater length in the next chapter on data analysis.

Grades

The first and simplest way to track incremental progress toward a long-term goal is to use a surrogate measure of performance. The most common surrogate for performance is the grade. While this data source is inexact, we make use of it every day as teachers. We all know that the ultimate evidence of student performance is the final exam or exit exhibition. However, from the day class begins until the final exam, we administer quizzes and tests, we assign homework, and we observe interim exhibitions for which we award grades. If you regularly grade students on work related to the achievement target that is the focus of your study, then the direction and pattern of those grades will provide you with good formative data on student performance. Grades, however, are just one form of interim data. Another method you may want to consider for tracking trends in performance is Rate of Growth Charts.

Rate of Growth Charting

As with the weekly time summaries discussed earlier, rate of growth charting invites the students to become partners in the data collection process. Rate of growth charting is built on the following set of assumptions:

- The teacher's goal is for each student to reach proficiency by the end of instruction.

- The teacher knows where the student is right now.

- It is possible to graph a rate at which a student needs to progress if he or she is to meet our high expectations.

Figure 3.7 (page 70) illustrates a rate of growth a first grader would need to maintain if she were to be ready for calculus by her senior year of high school.

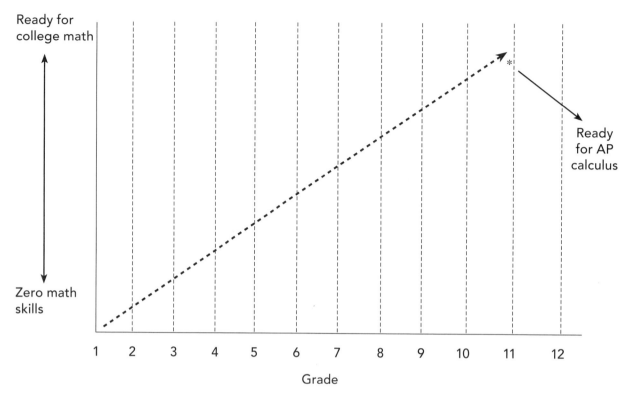

Figure 3.7: Rate of growth that will meet expectations.

One nice thing about rate of growth charting is that it doesn't take much teacher time. You can delegate to students much of the work involved in maintaining and analyzing their rate of growth. The process involves seven sequential steps.

1.   The PLC team meets and collaboratively examines two pieces of student work. The first is a product that reflects none of the skills you will be seeking to develop, and the second exemplifies everything you had hoped to achieve.

2.   The team brainstorms every subskill that needs to be obtained to move from a total lack of competence represented by the first piece of work to the exemplary performance (represented by the second piece). There must be at least nine subskills on the list brainstormed by the team.

3.   The group then reviews and edits the list until consensus is achieved. The list should contain *all* the essential subskills, from incompetence to extraordinary performance.

4.   Students are provided with a Rate of Growth Tracking Form and Rate of Growth Chart (pages 85–86) to be kept in their notebooks, portfolios, or some other accessible place. You should have the Rate of Growth Tracking Form preprinted with the complete list of subskills. You should provide one column on the bottom portion of the Rate of Growth Chart for each subskill identified by the team (step 2). In addition, create a timeline that corresponds to the duration of the project. The reproducible chart on page 85 has eighteen columns, or two per month for a nine-month school

year. You may need to adjust the number of columns to reflect the number of identified subskills and the actual duration of your project.

5. Whenever a student demonstrates acquisition of an identified subskill, the teacher places her initials next to that item on the Rate of Growth Tracking Form and writes the date.

6. Once the teacher has initialed a subskill on the Rate of Growth Tracking Form, the student colors in the corresponding column on the Rate of Growth Chart.

7. A quick look at the Rate of Growth Chart can then indicate whether the student is ahead, behind, or right on track to master all the necessary subskills prior to the end of the term (or the end of your study).

Rate-of-growth monitoring is a fun and efficient way to determine if a student is making adequate yearly progress toward hitting your priority achievement target.

Dated Records of Student Work Products

We all know there is no better record of what students have done or what they are capable of doing than the work they produce. For this reason, when conducting action research, many teachers make it a practice of saving (or having their students save) every piece of work completed. This can easily be accomplished by enacting a rule that every returned assignment is due back to the teacher (or classroom) along with a parent's signature no more than three days after the teacher returns it to the student. Additionally, I like to require that a student self-assessment be appended to the work. For purposes of student self-assessment, I use the four-question Student Work Product Self-Assessment Form (page 87).

By maintaining a chronological file that contains all of a student's work, along with your comments and their self-assessments, you will have at your fingertips a comprehensive record of each student's progress over the course of your project. This is a record that can be reviewed any time. If you have no need for further review of the student work products at the end of the term, you can simply return them to the students. The beauty of this data collection process is that it provides you with a huge amount of data and takes nearly no additional teacher time.

Data Collection Strategies for Impact Question 3: "What Was the Relationship Between My (Our) Actions and Changes in Performance?"

As noted earlier, it may not always be clear why student performance improved or declined. Although there is the potential to be fooled regarding the factors that trigger success, it isn't that difficult to develop confidence regarding what is contributing to student achievement. Learning rarely occurs in a vacuum. Both the teacher and the learner are in choice positions to observe what is happening whenever a student experiences success. Frequently, parents and other school staff are also witness to the growth process. The best way to validate what is influencing student performance is to seek data from those eyewitnesses. This is done by first reviewing all of the data obtained in response to Impact Question 2, "What improvement occurred for my (our) students?" and summarizing the findings. Once this has been done, it is time to consult the key eyewitnesses.

1.   Ask the students how they would explain documented trends in their performance on the target.

2.   Ask yourself how you would explain this change in performance.

3.   If applicable, ask the same question of the students' parents and another teacher.

There is no better source of information regarding what an individual knows, believes, or feels than his or her own testimony.

You might choose to collect eyewitness data in a number of different ways, ranging from the structured approaches of exit cards, surveys, interviews, or focus groups to a simple and rather informal process called member checking.

Leadership Note

Frequently, the only sources of data used to analyze student performance are standardized assessments or evaluations conducted exclusively by the teacher. Not only does this present limitations on the validity of any action research conducted, but also, by overlooking the student voice in assessment, we incur a lost opportunity cost. Whenever students are regularly asked to review and critique their own work, they become more engaged and committed to the learning process. Leaders can encourage the use of student voice and self-assessment in teachers' action research by asking the following questions whenever student performance is being discussed by teachers:

- How does the student assess his or her performance?

- What does the student think could have been improved?

Hearing these questions asked routinely will make it more likely that teacher researchers and PLC teams will decide to include student voices in their research.

Exit Cards

This quick and simple process can be done on a daily or weekly basis, depending on the length of your study. The completed exit card becomes the students' ticket to leave the room after class concludes. The exit cards are printed on index cards. What is asked on an exit card is up to the teacher. Minimally, the student is expected to provide his or her name and answer a question posed by the teacher—for example, "What did I learn today?" My preference is to use a card with two questions (fig. 3.8, page 73).

These cards provide me with instant feedback on what was learned and what my students credit as the cause of their success or confusion. Exit cards are a fast and efficient technique for any teacher to find out what his or her students are thinking and feeling.

```
┌─────────────────────────────────────────────────────────────┐
│  Name: _____          Date: _____      │
│                                                               │
│                        Exit Card                              │
│  What did I learn today? _____  │
│  _____    │
│  _____    │
│  _____    │
│  _____    │
│                                                               │
│  What helped me learn today? _____  │
│  _____    │
│  _____    │
│  _____    │
│  _____    │
│                                                               │
└─────────────────────────────────────────────────────────────┘
```

Figure 3.8: A sample student exit card.

Surveys

When designing a survey to solicit student, parent, or colleague perceptions, several guidelines should be followed.

- **Design questions to collect cognitive, affective, or opinion data as needed.** Surveys are quite versatile. You can use the survey to determine what a student knows (cognitive data), by asking something like, "Name five radioactive elements." Meanwhile, the same survey can be used to illuminate how the student is feeling (affective data), by asking, "How did you feel about studying the periodic table?" Finally, the same survey can be used to gather student opinion, using questions like the following: "Do you think learning about the structure of the periodic table was important for developing your understanding of chemistry?" Many teachers find they can construct a single survey that will elicit all three types of data.

- **Strive for brevity.** Like all researchers, PLC team members will soon realize that people are flattered when their ideas and opinions are solicited. But there is a limit to anyone's goodwill. People value their time and therefore appreciate short, concise surveys. If a survey takes more than ten minutes to complete, it is probably too long.

- **Strive for clarity.** You may get only one opportunity to ask your questions. If you construct an unclear and imprecise survey and later realize you need to revise your instrument and repeat the administration, your respondents will see the second request as an imposition. The way to avoid this is by conducting a mini–field test. Simply design your survey, and administer it to several people other than the intended respondents. Then check with the sample-survey takers to be sure each question was clear and unambiguous.

- **Consider confidentiality issues.** My recommendation to classroom teachers is to have students put their names on all surveys they complete. In my opinion, the benefits of being able to match attitudes and opinions with student demographics and the achievement data that you have been collecting (in response to Impact Questions 1 and 2) far outweigh any potential benefits of anonymity.

- **Consider disaggregation issues.** If, however, you elect to have surveys completed anonymously, you should first ask yourself an important question regarding how the data will ultimately be analyzed. Are there particular categories of students or groups whose responses you will want to compare? For example, will you want to see if the boys and girls perceived things similarly? Might those students who are relatively new to the school see things differently than the veterans? Given that our goal is universal student success, you will likely want to make these sorts of comparisons. If you decide to have a confidential survey and you want to examine equity issues, you will need to collect demographic data in place of names.

- **Don't lead respondents.** The power of a survey response is that it conveys the viewpoint of the respondent. However, that power is reduced and the credibility of the results is brought into question if it appears you were fishing for a specific response. For example, if you ask students to show their agreement with the statement, "Tardiness hurts academic performance," everyone would expect students to answer in the affirmative. But that doesn't mean that tardiness ought to rank at the top of a list of academic issues. A better way to elicit a response on this topic would be to ask the open-ended question, "Please list the things that harm academic performance," and then see how frequently tardiness is mentioned.

- **Use Likert scales**. A Likert scale allows respondents to choose a number that indicates their level of preference or agreement with a statement. This is a quick way to gather information on a number of topics, and the results are easy to aggregate. Consequently, these are very popular with busy action researchers. When using Likert scales, there are several additional issues to consider:

  - **Should you use a scale with an odd or even number of options?** Using a scale with an odd number of options (for example, three, five, seven) allows the respondents to select the middle number which is, in effect, a neutral or no opinion answer. Conversely, a scale with an even number of options (for example, two, four, six) is called a forced-choice scale, as it forces respondents to decide if they are more positive or negative about the issue. There is nothing inherently wrong in providing the "no opinion" option to your respondents; nevertheless, it is important to pause and consider whether you want to extend that option in advance.

- **Is there an opportunity for adding explanations?** As much as I've enjoyed the ease of use of Likert scales, they can leave me wondering what exactly a person meant by a response. For example, let's say I ask, "Using a 10-point scale, please rate my lecture on the functions of government." Four different students award a rating of 8. While I feel good that they all liked my lecture, this provides me with no help in improving my teaching in the future. However, if I asked the follow-up question, "What would it take to make it a 10?" I would likely receive some very valuable formative data.

- **When should you use multiple scales?** Often we want to know more than one thing about a phenomena, action, or event. For example, we might want to know how much students enjoyed something, while simultaneously finding out how valuable they thought it was. This can be done by creating a survey using multiple scales. I call these double Likert scale surveys. I have found them extremely useful for conducting class evaluations. The virtue of a survey with two scales is that it allows you to efficiently collect information on two phenomena at the same time. Figure 3.9 (pages 76–77) is an example of a double Likert scale survey designed to collect student feedback on a ten-day unit in high school biology.

I used this format periodically throughout the term in my own classroom. I would list every significant activity, assignment, or event done in class, and then ask the students to rate how much they enjoyed that experience, as well as how much they felt they gained from it. I have found that students will be quite honest in this format, and they easily discriminate between the two scales. Several times I have been alerted to an activity or assignment that wasn't rated as that much fun, but was nonetheless deemed beneficial. Likewise, I have had students alert me to fun activities that, in their opinion, weren't all that valuable.

Interviews

There may be numerous times when you will want to interview students as an action researcher. The virtue of the interview over the survey is that, while a survey will quickly and efficiently gather surface information, the interview, which is more time consuming, can go deep under the surface. Consequently, the choice between survey and interview is basically a question of breadth versus depth and fast versus time consuming.

The one circumstance when interviews are the preferable route for action research is when the focus of the study is an individual case or a comparative case study of a few select students. When conducting a case study, rather than collecting data from the entire class, the action researcher generally chooses to deeply examine the experience of a single or several representative students to better understand a phenomena. That deep examination almost always requires data obtained through interviews.

Classroom Activity	How much did I enjoy this?	How valuable was this?	Comments:
Discussion of the Requirements of Cells and the Functions of the Cell Membrane	1 2 3 4 5 6 7 8 9 10	1 2 3 4 5 6 7 8 9 10	
Pre-Laboratory Discussion of Osmosis in Elodea Cells	1 2 3 4 5 6 7 8 9 10	1 2 3 4 5 6 7 8 9 10	
Exploratory Activity: Osmosis in Elodea Cells	1 2 3 4 5 6 7 8 9 10	1 2 3 4 5 6 7 8 9 10	
Post-Laboratory Discussion	1 2 3 4 5 6 7 8 9 10	1 2 3 4 5 6 7 8 9 10	
Pre-Laboratory Discussion of Dynamic Equilibrium	1 2 3 4 5 6 7 8 9 10	1 2 3 4 5 6 7 8 9 10	
Exploratory Activity: Dynamic Equilibrium	1 2 3 4 5 6 7 8 9 10	1 2 3 4 5 6 7 8 9 10	
Post-Laboratory Discussion	1 2 3 4 5 6 7 8 9 10	1 2 3 4 5 6 7 8 9 10	
Pre-Laboratory Discussion of Factors Affecting Diffusion	1 2 3 4 5 6 7 8 9 10	1 2 3 4 5 6 7 8 9 10	
Exploratory Activity: Factors Affecting Diffusion, Part 1	1 2 3 4 5 6 7 8 9 10	1 2 3 4 5 6 7 8 9 10	

Classroom Activity	How much did I enjoy this?	How valuable was this?	Comments:
Exploratory Activity: Factors Affecting Diffusion, Part 2	1 2 3 4 5 6 7 8 9 10	1 2 3 4 5 6 7 8 9 10	
Post-Laboratory Discussion	1 2 3 4 5 6 7 8 9 10	1 2 3 4 5 6 7 8 9 10	
Pre-Laboratory Discussion of Osmosis	1 2 3 4 5 6 7 8 9 10	1 2 3 4 5 6 7 8 9 10	
Exploratory Activity: Osmosis	1 2 3 4 5 6 7 8 9 10	1 2 3 4 5 6 7 8 9 10	
Post-Laboratory Discussion	1 2 3 4 5 6 7 8 9 10	1 2 3 4 5 6 7 8 9 10	
Pre-Laboratory Discussion of Experimental Design	1 2 3 4 5 6 7 8 9 10	1 2 3 4 5 6 7 8 9 10	
Experiment: Osmosis and Blood Cells	1 2 3 4 5 6 7 8 9 10	1 2 3 4 5 6 7 8 9 10	
Post-Laboratory Discussion	1 2 3 4 5 6 7 8 9 10	1 2 3 4 5 6 7 8 9 10	
Review of Concepts	1 2 3 4 5 6 7 8 9 10	1 2 3 4 5 6 7 8 9 10	
End of Unit Quiz	1 2 3 4 5 6 7 8 9 10	1 2 3 4 5 6 7 8 9 10	

Figure 3.9: Ten-day unit on diffusion, osmosis, and cell membranes.

When conducting interviews, consider these guidelines:

- **Try to capture the data verbatim.** Interview data are rich, and much of their power lies in the precise words chosen by the respondent. Efforts to summarize answers inevitably result in a loss of much of the flavor of the response. Unless you are an extraordinary note taker, the best way to capture an interviewee's response verbatim is with a recording device. Of course, you should never record anyone without first acquiring that person's permission. My suggestion for all teachers conducting action research is to obtain advanced parental permission to record students' perceptions. While in my opinion this is not legally necessary, I feel it is the prudent thing to do. This matter is discussed at greater length in the appendix (page 145).

- **Establish rapport.** An interview will only be as good as the comfort level of the interviewee. Therefore, it is suggested that you begin the interview by chatting about a topic of mutual interest so interviewer and interviewee can get relaxed and comfortable with each other.

- **Create and follow an interview guide.** Rather than being governed by a rigid list of questions, structure an interview around an interview guide. This guide consists of topics that will be explored in the form of questions that are designed to encourage discussion. Your goal is to get the complete story and to be sure the interviewee has responded to everything in the interview guide. If, as it turns out, the interviewee answers multiple questions in a single response, there is no need for you to repeat the question. The purpose of the interview guide is to make sure that every area that needed exploration was explored with each respondent. To keep your interviews manageable, it is suggested that an interview guide be limited to no more than ten meaningful open-ended items.

- **Ask follow-up questions as needed.** When conducting an interview, you need not feel chained to a preordained protocol. If something intriguing comes up that calls for a follow-up question, ask away.

Focus Groups

A very common and productive way for teacher action researchers to gather information from their students is through structured focus groups. A focus group is basically a group interview, with some added benefits. In a focus group, individuals will often piggyback on answers provided by others. This allows the discussions to become richer and more free-flowing. The focus group is a time-efficient way to get a sampling of student perspective that goes deeper than a survey, yet isn't as time consuming or burdensome as conducting individual interviews. A number of considerations should be kept in mind when convening a focus group for classroom action research.

- **Make-up of group.** Consider whether you want the focus group to be representative of the class in its entirety or of a particular segment. Homogeneous groups tend to be more comfortable with each other, which leads to a good flow of ideas. Occasionally, teachers convene a series of separate homogenous focus groups. This way, each group is relaxed in the interview setting, and the researcher still ends up with an interview sample that represents the entire class. Another alternative is to make the focus group heterogeneous by creating a stratified sample. This is accomplished by listing each relevant category of students in the class (for example, boys, girls, high achievers, low achievers, middle achievers, low-income students, and students from advantaged families) and then inviting a person from each category to participate in each focus group.

- **Video and audio recording.** Recording focus group proceedings is very important because of the sheer speed at which participants share ideas. It is nearly impossible to take accurate notes in a dynamic focus group. A video record of focus group sessions ensures that when the results are transcribed, you will be able to identify exactly who was talking. As mentioned earlier, never record anyone without that person's prior knowledge and permission. Furthermore, you may consider it prudent to secure student and parental permission in advance (see the ethics discussion in the appendix, page 145).

- **Interview guide.** Rather than being governed by a rigid list of questions, the focus group session is structured around an interview guide. The guide is a list of the critical topics to be explored in the form of questions designed to encourage discussion. Your goal is to have a dynamic dialogue and to be sure that all participants have a chance to share their views on every issue covered by the interview guide. To keep your focus groups manageable, it is suggested that your interview guide contain no more than ten open-ended items.

- **Follow-up questions and polling.** When convening a focus group, you need not feel chained to a preordained protocol. If something intriguing is said that calls for a follow-up question, you should feel free to ask away. Furthermore, should someone express an interesting opinion, it is fully appropriate to go around the room and poll the attendees to see who agrees and who doesn't.

Member Checking

Member checking is an informal process used at the close of data collection to help validate findings. The process involves checking the data obtained and the conclusions drawn with the members of the group being studied. In the case of your action research, this means checking with the students and, where appropriate, other key eyewitnesses. The following five steps will enable you to quickly get a sense of eyewitness perceptions of the relationship between actions and outcomes.

1. Review the data obtained in response to Impact Question 2, "What improvement occurred for my (our) students?"

2. Ask yourself what you think explains these data.

3. Present your conclusions to the students and record their response using something like this simple prompt: "I noticed that your performance in _____ [improved/declined/was maintained] this term. What do you think most explains that?"

4.   Present your conclusions to someone else in a position to know your students' work (a parent, teacher's aid, teaching partner, and so on) and ask a similar question. Example: "I noticed that Rachel's work in _____ [improved/declined/was maintained] this term. What do you think most explains her performance?"

5.   Look for patterns in what you, the students, and other observers report in response to your queries. If you took specific actions in class that strongly influenced changes in student performance, they will likely surface through these discussions. For example, if the opportunity to work with a partner really helped Rachel achieve success, she will likely mention that as a factor that led to her improvement. You and her parents may have taken note of the same thing. When several independent respondents each attribute an outcome to the same factor, you can feel confident asserting that this factor appears to have made a big difference in producing the result.

Leadership Note

Most of the data collection techniques described in this chapter can be easily accommodated in the busy schedule of a classroom teacher. Unfortunately, while collecting the data may be rather easy, compiling and assembling the data can prove time consuming. For example, the design of a survey may be easily accomplished at a PLC team meeting and the administration of the questionnaire might only take a few moments of class time, yet aggregating the results can prove to be a labor-intensive task that will intrude on other important teacher work. Freeing up a few hours of clerical time to support PLC teams with this work is not a particularly expensive proposition, and it conveys to teachers that their school leaders care enough about the multiple demands on their finite time to relieve them of what are fundamentally clerical tasks.

Conclusion

We have now reviewed the development of three of the five habits of inquiry:

- Habit of Inquiry 1: Clarifying a Shared Vision for Success

- Habit of Inquiry 2: Articulating Theories of Action

- Habit of Inquiry 3: Acting Purposefully While Collecting Data

Once these habits have become a routine part of your practice, you will have become accustomed to clarifying what you wish to accomplish, it will have become natural for you to discuss the rationale behind your choice of actions (your theory of action), and you will have become comfortable collecting the data necessary to help you understand the influence of your actions on student achievement.

This brings us to the next chapter, where you will work on developing the ability to draw meaning from the data you are collecting.

Data Collection Planning Matrix

Use this form to organize your data collection when answering the three impact questions.

Project Focus:

Research Question	Data Source 1	Data Source 2	Data Source 3
What specifically did I (we) do?			
What improvement occurred for my (our) students?			
What was the relationship between my (our) actions and changes in performance?			

Pre-Intervention Time Expectation Worksheet

List the key actions or events you and the students expect to engage with, and estimate the average number of minutes per week of class time spent on this action.

Date: Class:

Actions (From Visual Theory of Action)	Approximate Class Time to Be Invested (in minutes per week)	Total Class Time to Be Invested During the Term	Comments	Percentage of Time to Be Invested

Weekly Time Use Worksheet

List the number of minutes for each category of action.

Category of Action	Week 1	Week 2	Week 3	Week 4	Week 5	Week 6	Week 7	Week 8	Week 9	Totals	Percentage of Time Used

Student Weekly Time Log

Distribute this form to students, and ask them to total how much time they spent during the week on each activity in column one.

Name:

Class:

Activity	Mon	Tue	Wed	Thurs	Fri

1) Please circle the number that indicates how hard you worked this week:

1   2   3   4   5   6   7   8   9   10

No Effort ←——————————————————→ Very Hard

2) What did you enjoy most about class this week (be as specific as possible)?

Rate of Growth Tracking Form

Students should keep a chart like this in their notebooks, preprinted with a complete list of the subskills that correspond to the project. Teachers initial the skill and add the date when the student demonstrates acquisition.

Student: _____   Achievement Target: _____

Subskills	Teacher's Initials	Date
1.		
2.		
3.		
4.		
5.		
6.		
7.		
8.		
9.		
10.		
11.		
12.		
13.		
14.		
15.		
16.		
17.		
18.		

Rate of Growth Chart

Provide students with a chart like this to keep in their notebooks, preprinted with a column for each of the subskills listed on the Rate of Growth Tracking Form and the timelines of the project (two per month in this example). Whenever a student demonstrates acquisition of a skill, the teacher initials that column and the student colors it in.

Student:

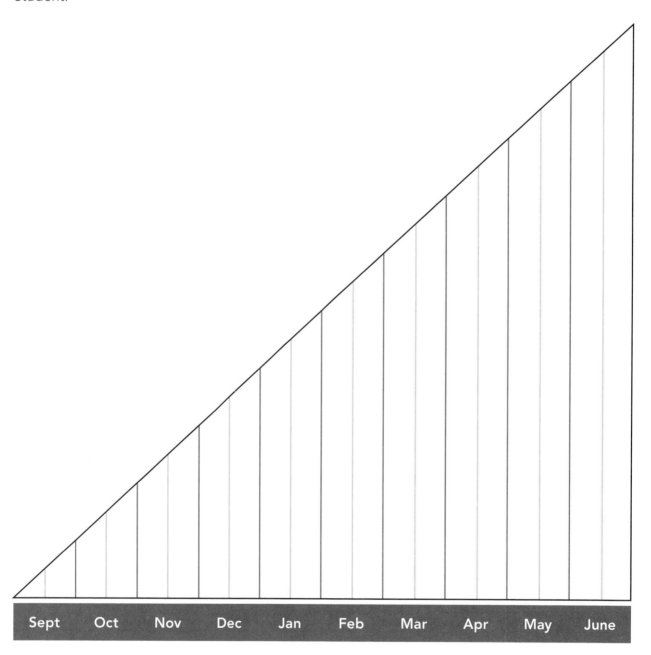

| Sept | Oct | Nov | Dec | Jan | Feb | Mar | Apr | May | June |

Student Work Product
Self-Assessment Form

Name: Date:

Work Product:

1. What did you like best about this piece of work?

2. What if anything made it superior to your previous best work?

3. What about this work could still be improved?

4. What did you learn by doing this particular piece of work?

Double Likert Scale Survey

Use this form to collect survey information about two aspects of a phenomena simultaneously.

Classroom Activity	How much did I enjoy this?	How valuable was this?	Comments:
	1 2 3 4 5 6 7 8 9 10	1 2 3 4 5 6 7 8 9 10	
	1 2 3 4 5 6 7 8 9 10	1 2 3 4 5 6 7 8 9 10	
	1 2 3 4 5 6 7 8 9 10	1 2 3 4 5 6 7 8 9 10	
	1 2 3 4 5 6 7 8 9 10	1 2 3 4 5 6 7 8 9 10	
	1 2 3 4 5 6 7 8 9 10	1 2 3 4 5 6 7 8 9 10	
	1 2 3 4 5 6 7 8 9 10	1 2 3 4 5 6 7 8 9 10	
	1 2 3 4 5 6 7 8 9 10	1 2 3 4 5 6 7 8 9 10	
	1 2 3 4 5 6 7 8 9 10	1 2 3 4 5 6 7 8 9 10	
	1 2 3 4 5 6 7 8 9 10	1 2 3 4 5 6 7 8 9 10	
	1 2 3 4 5 6 7 8 9 10	1 2 3 4 5 6 7 8 9 10	

Classroom Activity	How much did I enjoy this?	How valuable was this?	Comments:
	1 2 3 4 5 6 7 8 9 10	1 2 3 4 5 6 7 8 9 10	
	1 2 3 4 5 6 7 8 9 10	1 2 3 4 5 6 7 8 9 10	
	1 2 3 4 5 6 7 8 9 10	1 2 3 4 5 6 7 8 9 10	
	1 2 3 4 5 6 7 8 9 10	1 2 3 4 5 6 7 8 9 10	
	1 2 3 4 5 6 7 8 9 10	1 2 3 4 5 6 7 8 9 10	
	1 2 3 4 5 6 7 8 9 10	1 2 3 4 5 6 7 8 9 10	
	1 2 3 4 5 6 7 8 9 10	1 2 3 4 5 6 7 8 9 10	
	1 2 3 4 5 6 7 8 9 10	1 2 3 4 5 6 7 8 9 10	
	1 2 3 4 5 6 7 8 9 10	1 2 3 4 5 6 7 8 9 10	
	1 2 3 4 5 6 7 8 9 10	1 2 3 4 5 6 7 8 9 10	
	1 2 3 4 5 6 7 8 9 10	1 2 3 4 5 6 7 8 9 10	
	1 2 3 4 5 6 7 8 9 10	1 2 3 4 5 6 7 8 9 10	

Rate of Growth Summary Form

Use this form to enter content-coded data in preparation for electronic analysis.

1 Content Code	2 Pos-1/Neg-2	3 Narrative Comment	4 Name/ Subject-Code	5 Date

Codes:
1 Persuasion/campaigning
2 Writing
3 Brainstorming/thinking
4 Group work
5 Lobbying/mark-up

1 Content Code	2 Pos-1/Neg-2	3 Narrative Comment	4 Name/ Subject-Code	5 Date

Collaborative Action Research © 2010 Solution Tree Press • solution-tree.com
Visit **go.solution-tree.com/plcbooks** to download this page.

1 Content Code	2 Pos-1/Neg-2	3 Narrative Comment	4 Name/ Subject-Code	5 Date

Habit of Inquiry
Analyzing Data Collaboratively

Collaborative data analysis is the aspect of the collaborative action research process that I always find to be just plain fun! As you've been working through the action research process as outlined in this book, you have been engaged in the creative design work of the educational architect. You have been pursuing a shared vision that you value and implementing a theory of action that you believe in, while simultaneously collecting data on what has transpired in your midst. Now it is time for you to uncover the story buried in your data, to determine what it all means, and most important, to determine what you and your colleagues can learn from your bold exploration of terrain "where no one has gone before."

The actual procedures you will use to analyze your data will depend on both the data collected and the research question you are attempting to answer. Like action research itself, the process of data analysis can be engaged in by a single teacher working in isolation or by a collegial team. That being said, this is one of those circumstances where multiple minds will inevitably prove more insightful than one. For that reason, we will review data analysis as a collaborative process. If, however, you are working on an individual project and choose to conduct your analysis by yourself, the procedures you will use follow the same basic steps. When it comes to data analysis, we are developing a habit of inquiry that enables us to systematically look at all the available data on a phenomena and ponder, "What does this all mean?"

In this chapter, we will sequentially review the data you have collected to answer the three impact questions. We will explore data analysis by reviewing examples drawn from several micro-level (classroom) projects, as those are the inquiries most often engaged in by PLC teams. One product of your analysis will be sets of bulleted findings of fact produced in response to each impact question. At the close of the chapter, we will take a look at some minor adjustments you can make to the analysis process to make it more applicable to macro-level (schoolwide and programwide) projects.

Trend Analysis and the Three Impact Questions

The essential premise of educational action research is that our instructional actions—ours and our students'—have consequences for learning. The purpose of data analysis is to illuminate the connections and correlations between actions and outcomes in order to create a deeper understanding of those relationships. To accomplish this, we will follow a process similar to that used by historians to uncover the relationship between historical events: *trend analysis*. Trend analysis requires the historian to look at a phenomena—what in education we refer to as an *outcome* or what researchers call a dependent variable—over an extended period of time. Once changes in the dependent variable have been documented, the historian reviews the relevant circumstances, the independent variables, that may have changed or been manipulated during the period under study. The last step in trend analysis is to check to see if a correlation exists between the interventions and the outcomes obtained—that is, between the independent and dependent variables.

A powerful illustration of the use of this form of trend analysis is found in the realm of traffic safety. Figure 4.1 is a graph showing highway fatalities in the United States from 1988 to 1998. The figures indicate the number of fatalities per 100 million vehicle miles driven in the United States.

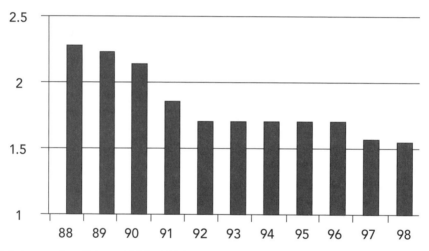

Figure 4.1: U.S. highway fatalities, 1988–1998.

Source: U.S. Department of Transportation, National Highway Traffic Safety Administration, 2001

It is clear that during this period, the rate of fatalities steadily declined. While that is a happy finding, taken by itself, it provides little direction to policymakers. Was this decline a random occurrence? Was it due to changes in highway design? Was it due to improvements in automobiles, improved driving, or something else? One way to determine the likely cause of the decline in fatalities is to graph the relevant actions that occurred (highway improvements, engineering improvements, driver education, and so on) against the fatality statistics. That is exactly what the National Highway Traffic Safety Administration did, and they came up with an interesting finding. Figure 4.2 indicates the rate of use of seatbelts during this same ten-year study period.

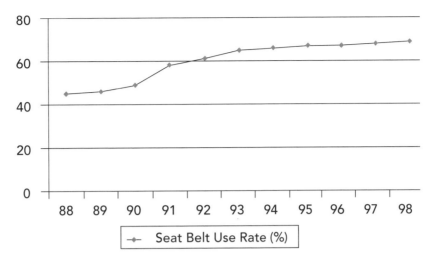

<u>Figure 4.2: U.S. seatbelt use, 1988–1998.</u>

Source: U.S. Department of Transportation, National Highway Traffic Safety Administration, 2001

When one examines these two trend lines side by side, one sees a clear correlation between increased seatbelt use and the outcome (lives saved). This finding led traffic safety experts to draw two important conclusions:

1. Seatbelt use saves lives.

2. It is good public policy to encourage seatbelt use.

As educational action researchers, we will be looking for similar types of correlations. Specifically, we will be looking for specific teaching strategies that correspond with improved student performance. We will begin this process by comparing the answers to the first two Impact Questions: "What specifically did I (we) do?" and "What improvement occurred for my (our) students?" However, it is critically important that our analysis not end at this point. As was pointed out in chapter 3, student and school performance can rise or fall independently of the purposeful actions we've undertaken. There is always the risk of overlooking an extraneous or intervening variable that could be the actual cause of an observed change. That risk will be addressed and mitigated through the analysis of the data collected in response to Impact Question 3, "What was the relationship between my (our) actions and changes in performance?"

Trend Analysis for Impact Question 1: "What Specifically Did I (We) Do?"

The work of the architect is captured in technical drawings and blueprints. These documents provide an accurate record for future reference. As you compile your answer to Impact Question 1, "What specifically did I (we) do?" you are creating an accurate record of the educational architecture you designed. The following set of practices will help you produce a record of what you did to help your students hit your achievement targets.

Generate a Timeline

In most cases, the unit of study for the action research conducted by PLC team members is the member's classroom or the performance of certain selected students. In such circumstances, the information contained in your edited lesson plan book will prove invaluable. The data analysis process begins with the construction of a detailed timeline containing all the major events and actions that your students experienced through your class. Using your edited lesson plans, you should be able to list, in chronological order, every instructional action that took place in your classroom. For the purpose of data analysis, an *instructional action* is defined as anything designed by the teacher with the intention of influencing student learning. This includes all classroom activities, such as media, assignments, lectures, quizzes, guest speakers, and cooperative learning experiences.

Proof Your Timeline

Once you've generated a chronological list, you will want to check it for comprehensiveness by doing one or more of the following:

- Put the list away for twenty-four hours, and then review it with fresh eyes. When you return to the list, try to recall anything you might have forgotten.

- Ask your students to write down everything they can remember doing or experiencing in class. Compare the student-developed lists to your own to see if the students recalled something you had forgotten.

- If you have a teaching partner, ask him or her to review your list to see if there were actions or activities he or she can recall that you failed to include on your list.

Once you have proofed the list of classroom actions, you will have created an instructional timeline built from raw data collected in response to Impact Question 1, "What specifically did I (we) do?" Sometimes you may feel that this is all that will be needed to answer this research question. Other times, especially when the list of instructional actions is long and the timeline appears overwhelming, you won't feel that the timeline alone effectively answers the question. In those cases, it can be helpful to reorganize the list by category. The process of categorizing instructional activities will only take a few minutes. These six simple steps will help you accomplish this.

1. **Review the list.** Review the list of actions looking for categories. A category is defined as a type of instructional activity that occurred more than once.

2. **Assign numbers.** Write down the categories, assigning a number to each one. For example:

1–Class discussions	5–Individual work (projects)	9–Reading
2–Reading responses	6–Jigsaw activity	10–Teacher lecture
3–Group work (projects)	7–Pair-share time	11–Videos
4–Guest speakers	8–Quizzes and tests	12–Worksheets

3. **Code the activities according to category.** Place the appropriate category number in front of each activity on your list of actions generated in step 1.

4. **Sort by category.** Sort the activities by category. Note: If you are using a table in a word-processing program or with a computer spreadsheet, you can use the SORT command to arrange your list in category order.

5. **Determine the totals.** Total the activities engaged in under each category.

6. **Summarize.** Write a set of bulleted statements summarizing the instructional activities that were most frequently engaged by you and your students.

Sample Findings From Instructional Timeline Analysis

The following list is a sample set of bulleted findings of fact derived from an instructional timeline generated in response to Impact Question 1, "What specifically did I (we) do?":

- The most frequently used classroom activity was cooperative learning.

- Thirty percent of instruction involved cooperative learning activities (including jigsaw, pair-share, and group projects).

- Students were involved in cooperative learning activities an average of three times per week.

- The second most frequent activity was the mini lecture (used fifteen times).

- Eight class periods were spent watching films and multimedia.

- Four class periods were spent working with guest speakers.

- Homework was assigned an average of three times per week.

- All homework assignments were followed by short-response essays.

- Study time was provided prior to each weekly quiz.

- Each student was assigned two individual projects.

- Each student participated in two major group projects.

A set of summary statements such as these is a concise way to summarize one's answer to Impact Question 1. Unfortunately, these data alone don't address whether the actions taken by you and your students were consistent with or divergent from the theory of action that you had developed earlier. However, you can determine the congruence of your actions with your theory by using the Weekly Time Use Summary Worksheet introduced in the last chapter (page 63) and following three additional steps. Figure 4.3 (page 98) contains a Weekly Time Use Summary Worksheet filled in by a hypothetical fifth grade teacher.

Category of Action	Week 1	Week 2	Week 3	Week 4	Week 5	Week 6	Week 7	Week 8	Week 9	Totals	Percentage of Time Use
Cooperative Learning	75	60	60	15	60	75	20	20	20	405	12%
Projects	0	0	90	150	150	90	150	150	75	855	27%
Guest Speakers/ Media	60	90	90	15	30	90	120	120	0	615	19%
Discussions	150	100	45	30	30	30	0	15	120	520	16%
Lecture	20	20	20	30	30	45	20	15	15	215	7%
Review	30	30	60	60	60	60	60	60	125	545	17%
Totals:	335	300	365	300	360	390	370	380	355	3155	98%

Figure 4.3: Sample weekly time use summary worksheet for a fifth-grade class.

1. Convert the percentages in the far right-hand column (actual time usage) into a pie graph, and compare these data with the graph illustrating anticipated time use that you constructed prior to data collection. Figure 4.4 (page 100) is an example of the fifth-grade teacher's anticipated time use contrasted with actual time use.

2. Write a set of bulleted summary statements, highlighting any significant differences you notice between the actual and anticipated use of time.

    For example, our hypothetical fifth-grade teacher might have noticed and written:

    *   I devoted less time to projects (27 percent) than I had anticipated (50 percent).

    *   I spent more time on review (17 percent) than I had anticipated (5 percent).

    *   I spent more time hosting guest speakers and using media (19 percent) than I had anticipated (10 percent).

3. Write a concise explanation of the rationale for any significant changes from your anticipated time use to actual time use. This fifth-grade teacher might have written:

    > Originally, I had assumed the students would produce six projects (three individual and three group projects). I had anticipated that guest speakers and media would occupy just 10 percent of our class time. As it turned out, my students enjoyed the stimulation of the speakers and media so much that I invited more speakers and added a feature-length film on the Civil War. As the term progressed, I found that each week I was using almost an entire period for quiz preparation and discussion. Those two decisions left less time for student projects, so I dropped one individual and one group project from the curriculum.

The two analyses discussed previously, the categorized teaching timeline and the summary graphs comparing the anticipated and actual time use, should produce enough evidence for you to confidently answer Impact Question 1, "What specifically did I (we) do?" Whether you use these methods or another one of your own invention, it is essential that, before proceeding any further into data analysis, you are able to state with precision the specific actions you and your students took during the period of this study in an effort to realize success with your target(s).

Trend Analysis for Impact Question 2: "What Improvement Occurred for My (Our) Students?"

The focus of Impact Question 2 is the essential justification for all of our work as teachers, action researchers, and PLC team members. Therefore, the accurate measurement and reporting of student growth and development are of utmost importance to all educational architects. There are two categories of student performance you may be concerned about:

1. Student achievement on objectives that are assessed on the state or provincial exam, either periodically or at the end of the school term

2. Student achievement on personally valued objectives that are not assessed on the state or provincial exam

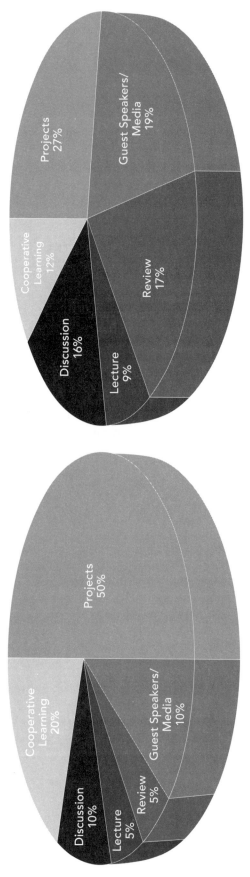

Figure 4.4: Sample pie graphs showing anticipated versus actual time use.

In either case, you will probably find reliance on a single end-of-year assessment to be unsatisfying; summative assessments can't help you identify specific actions that supported or hindered individual student growth. This is precisely the type of information you and your team need for your continued professional learning. However, examining formative data on student performance—specifically data that were collected while instruction was taking place—will enable you to surface satisfactory answers to Impact Question 2.

One nice feature of using formative data with the analysis of student performance is that you already possess a treasure trove of data that will prove helpful for their purpose. The first place to look is your gradebook. A second place to look is folders containing actual student work. In the last chapter, it was suggested that you maintain files of all the work completed by your students. As noted, one way teachers accomplish this is requiring that all completed student work be returned to the teacher or kept in a student-managed portfolio. Many teachers require students to return the work with a parent's signature within three days, or else the assignment is considered incomplete.

Your gradebook probably contains information on everything from attendance to quizzes, assignments, and tests. Consequently, your gradebook data should allow you to assess how each of your individual students progressed over the course of the term across a number of dimensions.

Disaggregate the Data

In most school districts, the assessment of student performance is done as a schoolwide or systemwide event. Once data have been collected and reported for the school district, they are further subdivided by school, by grade level, and ultimately by classroom. Reporting on individual student performance is frequently the last step in the process. Unfortunately, if the goal is improving instruction and fostering professional learning, the traditional model is upside down.

PLC teams who are using the action research model are encouraged to engage in the assessment process in reverse order. This new assessment paradigm, which is designed to maximize professional learning, begins with the assessment of individual students and then aggregates up, rather than the other way around. Figure 4.5 (page 102) illustrates the difference between the two assessment paradigms.

While we all recognize that every student is an individual, we also know that different categories of students have a tendency to experience school in different ways. This is frequently the result of prejudice or discrimination. For example, for many years, girls performed less well than boys in math and science, and in recent years, boys have underperformed girls in many academic areas. Children of poverty and students from underrepresented groups often experience school in a very different fashion than children from affluent mainstream homes. Furthermore, children with learning challenges will often respond differently to conventional instruction than other students. Bias can easily occur in our schools or classrooms without our even being aware of it. By aggregating and disaggregating our student data, we can reveal inequities that we may have been perpetuating unconsciously. This is why, as we engage in data analysis to more deeply understand our answer to Impact Question 2, "What improvement

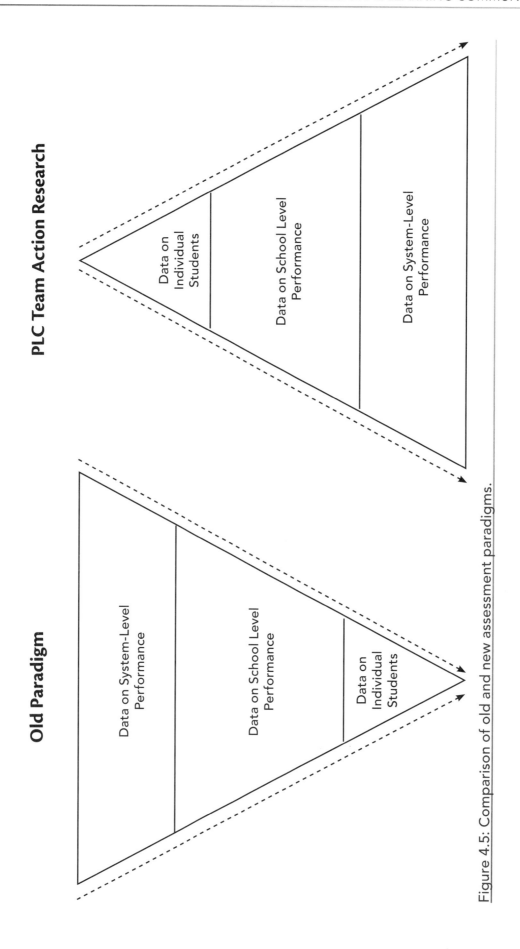

Figure 4.5: Comparison of old and new assessment paradigms.

occurred for my (our) students?" we will frequently want to compare and contrast the performance of students between and across demographic categories.

Generate Two Statistics Per Student

When trying to understand the dynamics of changes in student performance, it is worthwhile to generate two statistics for each student:

1. Level of performance achieved by the student (the average score obtained on quizzes, tests, and so on)

2. Growth demonstrated by the student (the difference between the student's scores at the beginning and end of instruction)

Figure 4.6 (page 104) shows a set of classroom data indicating level of performance and growth which is now ready for disaggregation, should the teacher so desire. In this example the teacher wanted to compare performance across three demographic variables (gender, past performance, and poverty). For purposes of her analysis, this teacher utilized the following criteria and definitions:

- **Growth**—This was determined by the difference between the average score on the first two quizzes and the student's average score at the end of the quarter.

- **Past performance**—For this analysis, students were grouped as high, mid, or low based on their previous year's grades. Highs had an A average, mids had a B or C average, and lows had a D or F average.

- **Poverty**—Students whose family income was at or below the federal poverty standard were considered to be in poverty.

After compiling this list, the teacher was able to sort her classroom data and summarize her key findings into a bulleted list with items like the following:

- The class average was 87 percent (highs averaged 91 percent; mids averaged 88 percent; lows averaged 80 percent).

- There was a gender difference, with the girls scoring an average of six points above the boys.

- Past high performers grew by an average of 1.5 percent.

- Past mid performers grew by an average of 5.5 percent.

- Past low performers grew by an average of 10.25 percent.

- The average score of students from low-income homes (82 percent) was seven points less than the students from advantaged homes (89 percent).

- The student with the greatest growth from January to March was Chris (twelve points).

- Ten out of sixteen students grew by five points or more.

- Average growth for the boys was seven points.

- Average growth for the girls was four points.

If you wish to create a data analysis form like the one shown in figure 4.6, use the blank version of this form (page 120). Alternatively, you could easily create your own table using a word processor or spreadsheet program. An advantage to using the computer for analyzing this type of data is the ease with which one is able to sort (disaggregate) and average data by column.

Use Rate of Growth Statistics

In the last chapter, we discussed using rate of growth charting to determine if students are progressing at a rate equal to, in excess of, or lower than your expectations. If you had your

Name	Average Grade	Growth	Gender	Past Performance	Poverty
Aaron	79	10	M	Low	yes
Angela	87	5	F	Mid	no
Belinda	90	5	F	Mid	no
Blair	85	6	M	Mid	no
Chris	83	12	M	Low	yes
Deirdre	92	3	F	High	no
Eduardo	90	0	M	High	yes
Melinda	89	7	F	Mid	no
Nora	92	2	F	High	no
Patti	89	4	F	Mid	yes
Peter	80	9	M	Low	yes
Quinn	87	8	M	Mid	no
Rhonda	90	5	F	Mid	no
Ricardo	89	4	M	Mid	no
Sam	78	10	M	Low	yes
Sara	91	1	F	High	no

Figure 4.6: Classroom data indicating average performance and growth.

students maintain Rate of Growth Charts (page 69), you could now summarize the data from those charts on a Rate of Growth Summary Form (page 121).

To determine where a student should be placed on the Rate of Growth Summary Form, do the following.

1. Count the total number of columns on the Rate of Growth Charts from the beginning of the study until the end of the data collection period, and divide by ten. The number you come up with equals a 10-percent increment.

2. Check to see how many 10-percent increments each student is either above or below expectations.

3. On the Rate of Growth Summary Form, indicate each student's rate of growth:

    * Adequate progress (no more than 10 percent above or below expectations)

    * Lagging (between 20 to 30 percent below expectations)

    * Excelling (more than 10 percent above expectations)

    * Deficient (more than 30 percent below expectations)

4. Once you have indicated each student's rate of growth, you may choose to aggregate the data using any demographic categories you are interested in monitoring. For example:

    * Boys and girls

    * Disadvantaged and advantaged

    * Historically low performers and historically high performers

5. Summarize the data in bullet format. For example:

    * The average rate of growth for boys in the class was *adequate*.

    * The average rate of growth for girls in the class was *excelling*.

    * Six of eight disadvantaged (free and reduced-price lunch) students were in the *deficient* category (75 percent).

    * One of eight disadvantaged students was in the *excelling* category (12.5 percent).

    * All but one of the ten historically low-performing students were either *lagging* or *deficient* (90 percent).

    * Nine of the ten historically high performers were in the *adequate* or *excelling* category; one high performer was in the *deficient* category (90 percent).

Trend Analysis for Impact Question 3: "What Was the Relationship Between My (Our) Actions and Changes in Performance?"

Hopefully, when analyzing the data on student performance, you uncovered evidence of positive growth. It is also possible that you uncovered performance that was troubling. Whether the findings that emerged were positive or less than positive, the question remains, How can you be sure whether it was your teaching or some other factor that was responsible for these changes? To better determine what influenced changes in student performance, it is necessary to complete the trend analysis that you began earlier in this chapter, while assembling data to answer Impact Question 1.

Complete the Trend Analysis

When you were analyzing data in response to Impact Question 1, you developed an instructional timeline (page 96). Now you will be plotting that data on a graph set up in the same manner as the one in figure 4.7.

The horizontal axis (with dates running from the start of your study until the conclusion of data collection) should correspond with the instructional timeline you completed. The vertical axis will be used for plotting student performance data. In the example are data plotting the weekly quiz scores for one student, Zach.

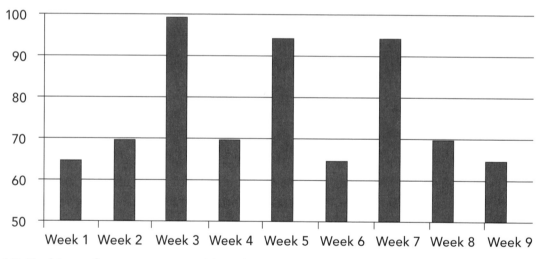

Figure 4.7: Zach's performance on weekly quizzes.

We can see by looking at the graph that, on average, Zach performed at the 70- to 75-percent level throughout the nine-week term. However, we can also note that he scored particularly well in weeks 3, 5, and 7 (90 to 100 percent). This raises some questions for his teacher. Was this coincidence, or did something specific happen in those three weeks that might explain his improved performance? The answer to this question should be relatively easy to uncover: Zach's teacher simply needs to refer back to her instructional timeline to ascertain if there was anything unique about those weeks. As it turns out, during each of those weeks, she had utilized a jigsaw activity and allowed the cooperative groups to conduct their own review for the Friday quiz. From the data, it appears that Zach responded far better to the collaborative process of quiz preparation than the whole-class discussion process that had been used the other six weeks.

This finding presented the teacher with another set of questions. Was Zach's performance representative of the class, or was he an outlier in his preference for collaborative study? Upon reflection, the teacher theorized that it probably was the active student involvement required with collaborative team study that made the difference for Zach. She was curious if the same thing might apply to other students in her class, and furthermore, she wondered if gender could be a factor. Figure 4.8 shows the average observed quiz scores for the entire class as well as the averages by gender. It appears that while not as pronounced, the trend in Zach's performance seemed to apply to the class as a whole. Furthermore, the positive impact of collaborative team study appeared to be more pronounced with the boys than the girls.

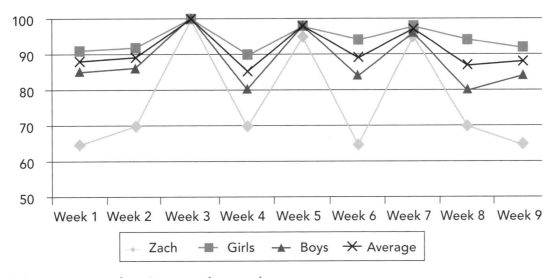

Figure 4.8: Average math quiz scores by gender.

Analyze the Narrative Data

The last set of techniques for data analysis that we will be discussing concerns making meaning out of qualitative narrative data. In all likelihood, much of the data you collected to answer Impact Question 3, "What was the relationship between my (our) actions and changes in performance?" was qualitative. It is also likely that the volume of this data (surveys, interview transcripts, exit cards, etc.) seems daunting. What follows is a generic strategy designed to help you analyze and sort through significant amounts of qualitative narrative data. If you had students complete surveys or exit cards, or participate in interviews or focus groups, you have collected data in the form of written material. In reality, there is virtually no limit to the types of material that can be subjected to narrative analysis. You might have instructional artifacts, such as handouts, tests, or quizzes; you might have copies of your comments on student work; or you might have the work-product assessments that students prepared in response to their own work. Each of these categories of data can be effectively analyzed using the same process.

The generic process that I suggest you use to analyze your qualitative data involves coding, sorting, and then placing the data into defined categories or bins (Miles & Huberman, 1994). Elsewhere (Sagor, 2000, 2005), I have contended that this approach to data analysis is similar to how one handles household recycling. For example, in my house, all the recyclables are stored in one location throughout the week. That corner of our garage evolves into an undifferentiated mass of cardboard, metal cans, glass jars, and newspapers. On Monday night, before the recyclers arrive, it is my job to sort this undifferentiated material into bins. In a matter of minutes, all the clear glass finds itself in one place, all the newsprint is consolidated, and the metal cans are together, as is the cardboard and miscellaneous paper. This quick and simple sorting reveals much about my family's consumption habits. For one thing, it is clear that we subscribe to far more papers than we read (the stack is high, neat, and filled with newspapers that have never been touched), and the volume of cardboard boxes we amass each week has me questioning the number of new products we routinely purchase.

Content Code the Data

We will now explore how you can use an analogous form of sorting and data analysis with the qualitative narrative data you have collected (surveys, interviews, focus groups, exit cards, teacher comments, work-product self-assessments, and so on).

The coding and data analysis process can either be completed mechanically (by hand) or, far more efficiently, with the use of a computer. Either way, the process has six steps.

1. **Review your raw data and theory of action.** It is suggested that you review the data by quickly skimming the material to get a sense of the nature of the responses. While you are skimming, be sure to have a pad of paper by your side so you can write down a word or a phrase that represents categories of repeated responses. Generate a new category once you notice the same phenomena being reported at least three times. The categories you identify will later become data "bins" (analogous to recycling bins) into which you will drop your data. For example, when reviewing students' exit cards, let's assume I begin noticing repeated comments regarding checking answers with peers, in-class review sessions, and parental pressure. As a result, each of these would become a category for use when sorting my data.

   I now look at my theory of action as illustrated on my priority pie and in the visual theory of action that guided this project. These documents are particularly important at this point in the analysis process because they will highlight for me the specific phenomena or factors that I believed, at the outset of the project, to be of greatest importance. Now I need to ask myself, "Are there slices of my pie or elements of my visual theory of action that should be added as categories or bins for the sorting of my data?" If I answer yes, then I should add those items to my tentative category list.

2. **Check your list of tentative categories with peers.** In most cases, you will not be the only member of your PLC team investigating student performance on a particular

target. Even when your theory of action differs from that of your colleagues (the alternative pilot project model), other members of your team will still share some of your perspectives on the target being studied. Therefore, it is suggested that you ask other members of your PLC team (or at least one of your colleagues) to review your tentative list of categories. Ask them if they think there are ways your data ought to be sorted that aren't included on your tentative category list. For example, let's return to the recycling metaphor. My recycler has asked me to separate my glass and metal cans into two separate bins. However, he has not asked me to distinguish between those glass and metal containers that once contained alcoholic beverages and the other containers. If it were important for me to document my family's alcohol consumption, I would be wise to sort my bottles and cans according to whether they had ever contained alcohol. This would require, of course, creating at least one additional bin.

3. **Identify your sources using subject codes.** Content coding is how you will identify and label each piece of pertinent data so it ends up in the appropriate "bin." Once you have finished content coding, sorting, and dividing up each piece of raw data, you may find that you want to know the origin of certain pieces of data. Knowing the source of information can be vitally important when making inferences and drawing conclusions from your data. The best way to ensure your ability to track the source of each piece of sorted data is to record three bits of information pertaining to each piece of data *before* it is placed into a bin.

    a. **Who provided the data?** In many cases, you will have the respondents' names. If so, simply attach a student's name to each piece of data before placing it into a bin. If you don't have a name, then you may want to include some demographic information. Many times, even if your data have been collected anonymously, you still obtained information (such as gender, past academic performance, years at school, and so on) from the respondents. If you have any demographic information regarding the source of a bit of data, you will want to record that information in a subject code and append it to the material before placing it inside a bin. Figure 4.9 shows an example of possible subject codes:

Gender:
- Male (A)
- Female (B)

Past performance:
- High performer (C)
- Mid performer (D)
- Low performer (E)

Years in school:
- Less than three years at school (F)
- More than three years at school (G)

Figure 4.9: Subject codes for student data.

Suppose a student had indicated on the survey that she was a female, middle-performing student who has been at our school for less than three years. I will want to note that whenever I make use of data obtained from her. I do this by applying a subject code to any data I use from her survey. If I found myself coding one of her responses, I would add the letters *BDF* (B for female, D for middle performer, and F for less than three years at our school).

In circumstances where you don't have names and you lack demographic information on your respondents, you should still assign a unique file number to every document (each survey filled out, each interview transcript, and so on). This is easily accomplished. Simply write a number at the top of each individual document, survey form, or interview transcript. Later, that file number will be attached to each piece of data that came from that document. This way, should the same or similar ideas surface multiple times, you will know if the response came from the same person or from multiple persons.

b. **The date the data were obtained (optional).** It is not important to collect all the data you are analyzing at the same time. However, should you be looking at data that were obtained over an extended period of time, such as exit cards, pre- and post-surveys, or weekly comments placed on student work, it will be important to note the date that the material was obtained. This information will enable you to discern trends occurring over time.

c. **The nature of the data (optional).** If all the narrative data you are analyzing came from the same place—such as interviews, your gradebook, or exit cards—then there is no need to note their origin. However, often during the analysis process, we find ourselves placing data obtained through multiple methods into the same set of bins. In those circumstances, you will find it helpful to note the source (for example: interview, survey, exit card, or student self-assessment).

4. **Content code the pertinent bits of data.** It is now time to go through all your narrative data (comments, exit cards, transcripts, and so on) and content code each pertinent piece of data. You may be asking at this point, "What makes a piece of data pertinent?" What makes a piece of data pertinent is that, in your opinion, it meets either of the following criteria:

- **Quantity.** A bit of data belongs inside one of your bins (categories) if it pertains to a repeated theme or category.

- **Quality.** A bit of data should be included in your analysis if, in your professional judgment, it seemed particularly meaningful. Often a thought or idea will only be mentioned once, or by one student, yet is so powerful that it is worth capturing in a report on your research.

Assign a number to each of the tentative categories on your list (derived in steps 1 and 2), and include an additional category for miscellaneous. This numbered list now becomes your content codes.

Re-read your raw data carefully. Whenever you find a quote or comment that pertains to one of your categories, write or type the appropriate content code at the start of the statement and underline the pertinent remark. If, in your opinion, a particular quote or comment belongs in several bins (categories), you may assign multiple content codes. For example, you might read an exit card comment saying, "My mother said that I should do a better job working with my classmates." If, upon reflection you conclude that this card belongs in two bins—the bin you created for *parental pressure* and the bin you created for *work with classmates*—then you should make a photocopy and code both the original and the copy. Remember, you don't have to content code every word, sentence, or paragraph in the data collected. You should only code the information that you assessed as pertinent.

Should you read a passage that appears incredibly interesting or moving (meeting the quality criterion), yet doesn't seem to belong in any of your bins (categories), you should content code it as miscellaneous and place it in your miscellaneous bin.

5.   **Assemble the data.** Should you choose to analyze your data electronically, using either a word-processing or spreadsheet program, it is suggested that you begin by creating a table similar to the one shown in the classroom data form (page 120).

Leadership Note

This particular task, entering content and subject coded data into a computer for further analysis, is extremely valuable, but it can be time consuming for anyone lacking excellent keyboarding or data-entry skills. Fortunately, for trained clerical personnel, it is quite simple to enter this information into a table. Offering clerical support to assist PLC teams with data entry is one of the best ways leadership can tangibly and symbolically demonstrate the value they place on the action research being conducted by the school's faculty. Helping with data entry costs very little, conveys a true sense of caring, and frees teachers to attend to other instructional tasks.

If you have decided to analyze your data mechanically (without a computer), there are two low-tech strategies for organizing content-coded data that you should consider using: cutting and sorting, and highlighting.

a.   **Cutting and sorting.** This strategy works best when the data being analyzed have been written on single-sided paper. Cut out each coded comment with scissors, being certain to note on the back of the comment *who* it came from (the student's name, subject code, and/or file number), the *date* the data were produced, the *source* of the data (exit card, teacher comment, survey, and so on), and whether the particular bit of data was positive or negative. Then, as with my curbside recycling, physically drop the coded comment into a pile, plastic bin, or manila envelope designated for that category. Should a single piece of data be coded as belonging in multiple categories, place a copy into each appropriate pile, bin, or envelope.

b. **Highlighting.** Assign a separate color to each bin (category). Read through your narrative data (surveys, interview transcripts, exit cards, and so on), highlighting each pertinent statement with the appropriate color.

Later, when the coded data are retyped, creating separate documents with all commonly coded data in the same document, be sure to note where each piece of coded data came from (by using the respondent's name, subject code, or file number).

6. **Analyze the data.** Once all the pertinent data have been coded and placed into either an electronic table, organized into a pile, dropped into a bin, or highlighted, it is time to figure out what it all means.

Once your content-coded data have been placed into the appropriate bins, you will find that many important findings will pop up automatically. The sheer volume of material in a bin is an indication of significance. If you typed your data into an electronic table, your computer will do the sorting for you. Whenever I do data analysis using an electronic table, I begin the process by selecting all the cells in the table and having my computer sort first by content code (column 1), then by nature of the comment (column 2), followed by name or subject code (column 4), and finally by date (column 5). Figure 4.10 (pages 113–116) contains data taken from exit card comments collected by a seventh-grade teacher after a legislative simulation unit in his twenty-seven-student social studies class. The exit card used by this teacher asked the students to report what they had learned from participating in the simulation.

By simply sorting and organizing his data by column, this teacher–researcher was able to tabulate the results and generate the following statements:

- Eight separate students (30 percent) mentioned the campaign as their favorite aspect of the unit.

- Four separate students (15 percent) reported a negative response to the campaign.

- Eight separate students (30 percent) mentioned the mark-up and lobbying process as a positive experience.

- Seven different students (26 percent) made reference to the value of the writing component of the unit.

- Five students (19 percent) made positive references to the brainstorming exercise, while one reported it as a waste of time.

- Five students (19 percent) mentioned group work as a positive experience. However, one student stated he would have rather worked alone.

- Two students, Sam and Jerry, reported the unit to be a negative experience overall.

1 Content Code	2 Pos-1/Neg-2	3 Narrative Comment	4 Name/ Subject Code	5 Date
1	1	I didn't agree with the teachers' rights bill until I read the voter's pamphlet.	Adam	
1	1	I realized the importance of compromise.	Blair	
1	1	I learned that you have to work on some things that don't matter to you to get other people to support your ideas.	Brandon	
1	1	I learned how hard it was to get and keep a majority.	Emma	
1	1	I learned a lot preparing the campaign with my team.	Jeff	
1	1	I liked working with Juan and Maria on the campaign.	Joey	
1	1	It's hard to change someone's mind. You have to give something if you want to get something.	Rebecca	
1	1	That I enjoyed campaigning	Sara	
1	2	I learned from the campaign that some people aren't willing to compromise on anything.	Michelle	

Codes:
   1 Persuasion/campaigning
   2 Writing
   3 Brainstorming/thinking
   4 Group work
   5 Lobbying/mark-up

Figure 4.10: Data collected from exit card comments of a seventh-grade social studies class.

continued ➡

1 Content Code	2 Pos-1/Neg-2	3 Narrative Comment	4 Name/ Subject Code	5 Date
1	2	I hated the campaign. People just shouted at each other.	Rachel	
1	2	I learned how much I hate to compromise.	Rachel	
1	2	The campaign wasn't fair. I never got to share my opinion.	Ron	
1	2	I didn't like trading for positions on votes.	Sam	
2	1	I liked writing the Student Rights Bill.	Donna	
2	1	Writing the bill was tougher than I thought. But I learned a lot from it.	Hailey	
2	1	Creating the written arguments was the best part of the class.	Juan	
2	1	The meaning of words matters, and you have to be precise.	Michelle	
2	1	To learn to write using clear language	Marcus	
2	1	I didn't enjoy writing the voter's pamphlet, but that helped me with my writing.	Michelle	
2	1	I didn't agree with the teachers' rights bill until I read the voter's pamphlet.	Adam	
3	1	It was helpful to spend time thinking about our rights.	Angela	
3	1	I learned from the brainstorming with my team.	Maria	

1 Content Code	2 Pos-1/Neg-2	3 Narrative Comment	4 Name/Subject Code	5 Date
3	1	I learned you need to be sure of your arguments before starting a debate.	Ricardo	
3	1	By brainstorming I learned that teachers need rights just like students do.	Zach	
3	2	I didn't learn anything from my group. The brainstorming was a waste of time.	Sam	
4	1	I learned a lot working with the other lobbyists.	Beth	
4	1	I learned from the brainstorming with my team.	Maria	
4	1	Our team was the best.	Jamie	
4	1	I learned a lot preparing the campaign with my team.	Jeff	
4	1	I liked working with Juan and Maria on the campaign.	Joey	
4	2	I would have rather worked by myself.	Sam	
5	1	I learned a lot when we marked up the bill.	Emma	
5	1	Realizing that the final bill can be so different from the original	Amy	
5	1	I learned a lot working with the other lobbyists.	Beth	
5	1	The lobbyists were really helpful.	Janis	

continued ➡

1 Content Code	2 Pos-1/Neg-2	3 Narrative Comment	4 Name/ Subject Code	5 Date
5	1	I liked marking up the bill.	Jon	
5	1	I learned bills change. I didn't even recognize my own ideas after our bill had been amended.	Ricardo	
5	1	I learned how to lobby for amendments.	Sara	
5	1	I learned that bills change as they go through the process of becoming laws.	Shauna	
6	2	The government always does what it wants anyway. This stuff is bull.	Jerry	
6	2	I hate social studies.	Sam	

This very same analysis of exit card data could also have been accomplished mechanically with the use of the cut-and-sort or highlighting strategy. This is accomplished by following these three steps:

a. Take each pile, bin, or envelope and sort the pieces of data by nature of the comment (positive or negative).

b. After you have completed that initial sort, sort each stack by name, subject code, date (when applicable), and source.

c. After the second sort is complete, summarize the findings from each of the piles with bulleted statements.

The bulleted statements of findings you generate through the analysis of qualitative narrative data and the findings from your trend analysis should provide a satisfying answer to Impact Question 3, "What was the relationship between my (our) actions and changes in performance?"

Analysis at the Macro Level

With a few notable exceptions, the steps and processes for analysis just described will work as well at the macro (schoolwide or programwide) level as they do at the micro level. As a result of their broad focus, macro-level projects frequently result in more data being assembled from more subjects. Fortunately, with schoolwide projects, there generally are also more people on the research team who can assist with the analysis process. This is fortunate, since with schoolwide or programwide projects we will generally want to subject our data to further analysis by sorting out the additional variables of grade level, GPA, and classroom assignment.

Conducting Data Analysis as Teams

One indicator of a school that has been transformed itself into a professional learning community is that micro-level action research is occurring all the time. Being a committed team of professionals, the educators in these schools exhibit a continuous curiosity about the operation of their programs and the educational experience of their students. It is this curiosity that gives rise to all the classroom-based inquiries. One major problem with micro-level action research projects is that it is hard to divide up the labor; in that respect, the schoolwide and programwide projects have an advantage: with macro-level projects, there are usually more people to share the load. This is particularly helpful when doing data analysis, since it is rarely necessary for everyone to be engaged with every aspect of the analysis process. But while everyone doesn't have to sort and analyze each piece of data, a certain level of group involvement is necessary to ensure that the results of the research are valid, reliable, and worthy of our confidence.

The following three steps will help ensure that a schoolwide or programwide team, charged with conducting a macro-level action research project, will end up happy with the results of its collaborative data analysis.

1. **Conduct periodic member checking of findings.** As noted earlier, researchers often use member checking to further validate their findings. This involves asking the people in the best position to know the story embedded in the data (the members of the study population) to react to the tentative findings. Action researchers conducting schoolwide or programwide projects will want to conduct member checking several times during the analysis process:

    *   After generating bulleted findings in response to Impact Question 1, "What specifically did I (we) do?"

    *   After generating bulleted findings in response to Impact Question 2, "What improvement occurred for my (our) students?"

When a collaborative action research team or the team's analysis subcommittee believes they have generated an adequate answer to one of the first two Impact Questions, it should return to either the full team or go to a larger faculty group to present the preliminary findings. When doing this, only the bulleted findings should be shared. The team should avoid lengthy explanations or extensive elaboration. The purpose of the team presentation should be straightforward and simple: to report the preliminary findings of fact. A statement such as the following is made to introduce the issue: "Based upon our preliminary analysis of the data, this is what we found." Once the findings of fact have been presented, this question and request should follow:

- Are you aware of any findings that were omitted or data that we may have misunderstood?

- If so, please share what you feel was left out or misunderstood.

The responses of colleagues to those two questions should be collected in writing. Based on this feedback, the team or analysis subcommittee may elect to reconsider its preliminary findings. However, the fact that during member checking some colleagues did not concur with the findings does not, in itself, obligate the team to change their conclusions.

As a committee of professionals, you should be comfortable owning both your research and the reasoning that informed your findings. If, through member checking, the team discovers a discordant opinion, yet elects to maintain its findings as originally written, then the team simply needs to acknowledge in its final report that a dissenting perspective had surfaced and was considered and give the rationale behind the team's decision to maintain its original position. (There is an extensive discussion on the reporting of research in the next chapter.)

2. **Consider the variables of grade level, GPA, and classroom.** Historically student success has not been distributed equitably in our society. The underperformance of certain categories of students is frequently the result of conscious or unconscious actions that can be changed. For this reason, whenever you conduct action research you should analyze the data in a way that highlights inequitable patterns of performance. This is why, when the focus is on schoolwide or programwide initiatives, it is important to disaggregate student data by two additional variables.

   a. **Grade level**—Students inevitably grow and develop as they proceed through school. Consequently, when we are seeking to completely understand the students' experience as they move through our programs or as they progress from grade to grade, it is helpful to sort and compare data across grade levels.

   b. **GPA**—Many things at school are experienced differently based on a student's past academic history. Often, social and academic status are factors of a student's past academic performance. For this reason, students who are perceived as having differing academic status often see the school and its programs quite differently. Furthermore, all things being equal, students will continue to perform as they had been performing. By disaggregating student responses in accordance with their past academic performance, we will be able to uncover these different perspectives. This type of disaggregation is easily accomplished. In secondary schools, it is easy to code students by their past academic performance using the school-computed grade point average (GPA). At the elementary level, student self-reports can substitute for the grade point average. I have found that elementary students are able to inform us of their perceived academic status; the teacher has only to ask the students to compare their skills with the rest of their class in a subject that the teacher feels is a good indicator of overall academic proficiency. Generally, I use math. I simply ask the students, "Compared to your classmates, are you among the best in math, are you an average math student, or are your math skills below your classmates?"

3. **Code the narrative data.** The process for coding and analyzing narrative data is the same as described earlier in this chapter. However, when a team is conducting a macro-level project, not everyone on the team needs to be involved in the review and content coding of data. When coding a large quantity of data for a macro-level project, it is suggested that a team organize the work as follows:

   - Solicit everyone's input regarding potential content codes.

   - Have at least three individuals code all the raw data. As a rule of thumb, an item needs to be deemed pertinent by at least two of the three reviewers to be placed into a bin.

   - When a list of tentative findings is produced, member check the findings with the entire study committee.

Conclusion

This brings us to the end of our discussion of practices that build Habit of Inquiry 4, Analyzing Data Collaboratively. In the next chapter, we shall address the fifth and final step of the collaborative action research process, Habit of Inquiry 5, Using Informed Team Action Planning. This is the part of the process where you will look at taking your findings of fact and using them to produce credible conclusions that will help you creatively design meaningful improvements for your programs or classrooms.

Classroom Data Indicating Average Performance and Growth

Use this form to assemble classroom data for disaggregation.

Name	Average Grade	Growth	Gender	Past Performance	Poverty

Rate of Growth Summary Form

Use this form to summarize the data from students' Rate of Growth Charts.

Name	Deficient	Lagging	Adequate Progress	Excelling

Habit of Inquiry
Using Informed Team
Action Planning

Having completed the process of data analysis, you should be feeling very good about yourself. You and your team have come a long way and are now ready to get to work on the final habit of inquiry. As a team of educational architects and as a community of dedicated professionals, you have nearly completed your journey and will soon be arriving at your desired destination. When you exercised Habit of Inquiry 1, Clarifying a Shared Vision for Success, you engaged in the first act of the educational architect—you imagined something that hadn't previously existed. As you practiced Habit of Inquiry 2, Articulating Theories of Action, you applied your best thinking, the wisdom you gained from experience and your knowledge of the field, to the design of a novel approach to getting you to the elusive destination you had dreamed of reaching. To accomplish this, you engaged in the creative design work required of educational architects. You prepared a theory of action that you had good reason to believe would be successful in getting you and your students to the ultimate outcome of universal student success. Then, you employed the skills of Habit of Inquiry 3, Acting Purposefully While Collecting Data, to implement and assess your theory of action.

Like educational architects, the designers of computer software use their theories of action to create prototype software. Once they have developed what clearly appears (on the surface) to be a good product, they assess their prototype in what are called beta tests. The same practice is used by designers of automobiles and airplanes. The prototype vehicles they design are put through their paces by outstanding test pilots and drivers who test the products and critique every aspect of the innovative prototypes. You have now done the same thing with your creative educational architecture. Your prototype, your theory of action, has now been field tested by the best conceivable test pilots, people who know and understand the theory, the prototype, and the students it was designed to serve, better than anyone else. Your theory of action was tested by you, your colleagues, in your school, with your students.

Finally, you practiced Habit of Inquiry 4, Analyzing Data Collaboratively, to probe the data and produce findings of fact in response to three essential questions about the effectiveness of your prototype. It is now time to draw conclusions from your field test, fine-tune your prototype, and prepare it for implementation.

Understanding Action Planning

The key question you and the PLC team are facing at this juncture is, "Given what has been learned about our theories of action, what should we do differently next time?" This is accomplished by following a three-step process.

1. Review your pre-intervention theory (or theories) of action.

2. Review the findings from each person's data.

3. Revise the original theory (or theories) of action based upon the findings.

There are two routes that PLC teams may have traveled to get to this stage of the action research process. In some cases, the entire team pursued a single theory of action while collecting data in their individual classrooms. In other cases, the PLC team discovered that its members held divergent professional perspectives on how to achieve universal success, and as a consequence, different team members pursued different theories of action. In the latter case, the collaborative action research became a test of alternative pilot projects.

In either case, the three-step process that will help you internalize Habit of Inquiry 5, Using Informed Team Action Planning, operates in fundamentally the same manner. In this chapter, we will examine several strategies for your consideration when pursuing the three-step planning process. The chapter will conclude with a discussion of alternative approaches for sharing PLC team action research.

Step 1. Review Your Pre-Intervention Theory (or Theories) of Action

On the wall of your meeting room, display a poster-sized copy of each visual theory of action that was prepared prior to beginning instruction or implementation of the intervention, and make copies of these visuals for each member of the team. If your team examined alternative pilot projects, each team member should also have available a copy of the visual theory of action that he or she personally implemented.

Keep in mind that the visual theories of action the members are now looking at represent how you or they expected things would play out before action commenced. Now that you have had a chance to implement the theory, it is time to examine the original visual theories of action retrospectively. Slowly walk through the visual, seeking out and reflecting on things that may have worked out differently than you had originally anticipated. Make a note of anything significant that occurred that wasn't referenced on your original visual theory of action.

Then adjust your visual theory of action so it accurately represents what actually transpired. This might mean deleting actions and events that never took place or adding pertinent events and actions that might have occurred yet weren't included in your original theory. Once this has been accomplished, you will have produced what we will call an *operant theory of action*. The operant theory is an accurate representation of the actions that were "in operation" when the study was conducted. Occasionally, we find that an initiative that several PLC team members were going to implement in the same way ended up being implemented in substantially different ways by different members. When this occurs, a separate operant theory of action should be drawn for each of the different approaches.

Step 2. Review the Findings From Each Person's Data

This step involves all the team members who were working toward success on the same achievement target, even if they were following different theories of action. Going question by question, each member reads through the bulleted findings of fact from his or her field test. (The preparation of bulleted findings was discussed in chapter 4, page 97.) This is similar to a test pilot debriefing with the aid of a personally authored flight journal. Once all the findings of fact have been read, the group proceeds to ask itself the following questions:

- Are these findings clear?

- Are there other pertinent findings (supportable by data) that have not been included?

We will now examine how a PLC team might respond to these questions while reviewing their findings one Impact Question at a time.

Review of Impact Question 1: "What Specifically Did I (We) Do?"

You should have already made adjustments to the original visual theory of action(s) based upon your experience (step 1). What resulted were your operant theories of action. Now as you are sharing the findings, your group may realize that fundamentally different things occurred in different classrooms. This doesn't necessarily indicate that anything went wrong; rather, it could mean there was something fundamentally different about the context of the two classrooms. The action research process as described in this book has largely focused on making technical adjustments to issues of classroom and instructional organization. This provides valuable professional learning, yet we know that classroom and instructional organization are not the only factors that influence student learning. Matters of personal style, teacher personality, and classroom chemistry also powerfully influence student performance. Research that doesn't take this into account is research that is not portraying the reality of the classroom experience. This is why the production of multiple operant theories of action to accurately reflect the instruction experienced in each classroom is so important.

Once all the operant theories have been articulated, the PLC team will be able to assert with confidence that it fully understands any differences between what had been proposed (the pre-intervention theories of action) and what was delivered (the operant theories of action).

The essential question that Habit of Inquiry 5 asks us to ponder is: "How should our team's future plans be adjusted?" We cannot adequately answer that question quite yet. Before determining whether our pre-intervention theory of action, our operant theory of action, or any other theory should govern our actions in the future, the team must first determine how satisfied they are with their findings of fact in response to Impact Questions 2 and 3.

Review of Impact Question 2: "What Improvement Occurred for My (Our) Students?"

Using the Findings Comparison Chart (page 137), write down each bulleted finding pertaining to student performance that was noted in response to Impact Question 2, and indicate in which classrooms that finding was made. Prepare a separate chart for each operant theory and only include findings from members who followed that operant theory of action.

Using the information from each Findings Comparison Chart, write a composite set of bulleted findings for Impact Question 2. This is a set of findings that you—as a group of professionals who implemented the same operant theory—are prepared to say constitute an accurate presentation of what was learned about improving student performance through your study. The following is a sample set of composite findings:

- In four of five rooms (80 percent), every demographic group of students demonstrated growth in writing performance. In one room, two groups—the male students and the students possessing weak academic histories—showed no growth.

- In all five classrooms (100 percent), the scores earned by the girls exceeded that of the boys.

- In all five classrooms (100 percent), the greatest rate of growth was achieved by the students who had been low performers.

- In four of the five classes (80 percent), the lowest-performing group was the students who had been low performers in the past.

Review of Impact Question 3: "What Was the Relationship Between My (Our) Actions and Changes in Performance?"

Each member shares with colleagues who implemented the same operant theory of action his or her set of bulleted findings in response to Impact Question 3. Using an impact table like the one in figure 5.1 (page 127), track these findings regarding the relationship between instructional action and performance across different classrooms. This is done by considering each finding (that speaks to a specific instructional action) and then seeing in which classrooms that same finding applied. Note that findings regarding performance can include changes in attitude and beliefs as well as academic achievement.

Data Source	Cooperative Learning	Simulation #1	Simulation #2	Independent Research Project
Grades		Average grades earned: Room A: 87% Room B: 82% Room C: 80% Room D: 82% Room E: 79%	Average grades earned: Room A: 95% Room B: 90% Room C: 90% Room D: 89% Room E: 85%	Average grades earned: Room A: 85% Room B: 80% Room C: 80% Room D: 79% Room E: 82%
Student Survey	Cooperative learning reported to be "helpful" or "very helpful": Room A: 100% Room B: 75% Room C: 80% Room D: 70% Room E: 90%	Students reported learning the most from Simulation #1 (found in rooms A, B, C, D, and E).		Students reporting the IR project to be "helpful or very helpful": Room A: 65% Room B: 60% Room C: 67% Room D: 59% Room E: 61%
				Percent of "high achievers" rating the IR project as "helpful or very helpful": Room A: 90% Room B: 95% Room C: 90% Room D: 90% Room E: 93%

Figure 5.1: A partially completed impact table.

Following is a sample of composite findings that a PLC team could generate from the limited data contained in figure 5.1:

- Survey responses showed that the majority of students in all five classes felt that they learned the most from the first simulation.

- More than two-thirds of the students in four of the classrooms perceived cooperative learning activities to be helpful or very helpful. One hundred percent of the students in one of the classrooms reported cooperative learning to be very helpful.

- In all five classes, the average grade earned for the second simulation was higher than the first simulation.

- In all five classes, significant disagreement existed on whether the independent research project was valuable.

- In all five classes, the independent research project was rated higher by those students with strong academic histories than by the other students.

Once you and your colleagues have finished entering your findings onto the impact table, write a set of composite bulleted findings in response to Impact Question 3. A blank Impact Table can be found on page 139.

Step 3. Revise the Original Theory (or Theories) of Action Based Upon the Findings

As a team of educational architects, it is now time for you to make the necessary modifications to your preliminary design and prepare it for the next round of implementation. At this point, you have field tested an operant theory (or theories) of action and systematically analyzed multiple sets of data on the effectiveness of that theory (or theories). Perhaps everything worked perfectly and each student reached high levels of proficiency on every achievement target. In the rare circumstances when this occurs, the wise thing is to follow this same operant theory of action in the future. After all, if you keep doing what you've been doing, you will likely keep getting what you've been getting! If this happened and you and your team produced universal student success, you can proudly assert:

> As a result of our research, our team now has sound reason to believe that our operant theory, as illustrated by the attached visual theory of action, will produce success for all students. Therefore, it is our recommendation that this theory of action be followed in the future.

However, more frequently, based upon an analysis of data, you will conclude that your prototype, although probably very good, still needs some tweaking in order to produce universal student success. This is quite similar to the research and development efforts that occur in most other professions. It is rare in any field that a prototype goes to market without further refinement. In fact, prototypes generally go through several cycles of testing to ensure an effective final product.

Creating a New and Improved Theory

The suggested process for revising your operant theory of action and transforming it into a viable plan for the future consists of six steps. The first four will enable a PLC team that worked from a single operant theory to turn their findings into a new and improved theory. In cases where the project involved multiple operant theories (the alternative pilot project model), two additional steps must be added to the planning process. The steps of the planning process are:

1. **Contrast anticipated and actual time use**. Many readers will have already completed this task as part of their data analysis. If you completed this step, this is a good time to once again compare and contrast the differences between how you anticipated using your time and the way you actually spent it during the project. Make note of any differences between the time you thought the project would take and the time it actually took.

2. **Create a new priority pie**. Using the Projected Time Use Form (page 138), you should now create a new projected time use priority pie. This is done as a group

activity. When you prepared your first projected time use priority pie (as part of your initial theory development), the percentages used were based upon your best hunches; this time the pie graph should be a more accurate representation of reality, since this time it is being informed by both your best hunches *and* the wisdom gained through your research.

3. **Review the operant visual theories of action.** Place copies of the operant visual theories of action on the wall, and make copies for each participant. These graphic reconstructions represent what students have actually been experiencing in your classrooms. Carefully review each of these theories of action.

4. **Construct a revised visual theory of action.** Post a large blank piece of chart paper next to the picture of each operant theory of action. Giving consideration to the weight of the independent variables (your newly created priority pies in step 2) and the findings of your research, redraw a visual theory of action to accurately reflect the actions your team now believes should be taken the next time you work on this achievement target. These two graphics constitute the equivalent of before and after pictures: the first one, the operant theory, illustrates the actions taken before data analysis, and the second, the revised visual theory of action, drawn after data analysis, reflects your proposal for action in the future.

Figure 5.2 (page 130) illustrates an operant theory of action contrasted with a revised visual theory of action, fig. 5.3 (page 131), that was drafted after action research data had been analyzed. In this case, the desired outcome was for the students to hit two achievement targets. The team wanted the students to learn how to (1) contribute to meaningful collaborative work, and (2) produce quality group multimedia projects. Through data analysis, two powerful findings emerged. The operant visual theory of action reflected a strategy of randomly assigning students to cooperative groups and empowering those groups by allowing the students to choose the focus for their group projects. The team's analysis of the data revealed that both of these instructional decisions were problematic. Therefore, in the future, the teachers decided that their instructional plan should include (1) strategically grouping the students, and (2) providing students with greater teacher direction in the selection of project topics.

An examination of the two theories of action will reveal that the new and improved theory contains two significant changes from the operant theory.

a. The strategic grouping and regrouping will be based on assessment data.

b. Students are now required to negotiate their work plans with the teacher.

In circumstances when the members of the PLC team pursued multiple operant theories of action (the alternative pilot project model), the action planning process should include two additional steps (steps 5 and 6).

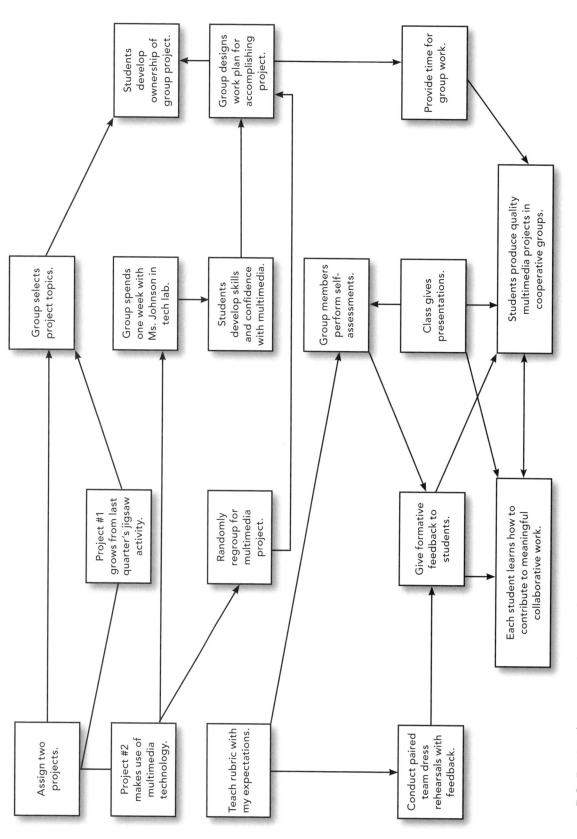

Figure 5.2: Revised operant theory of action after research.

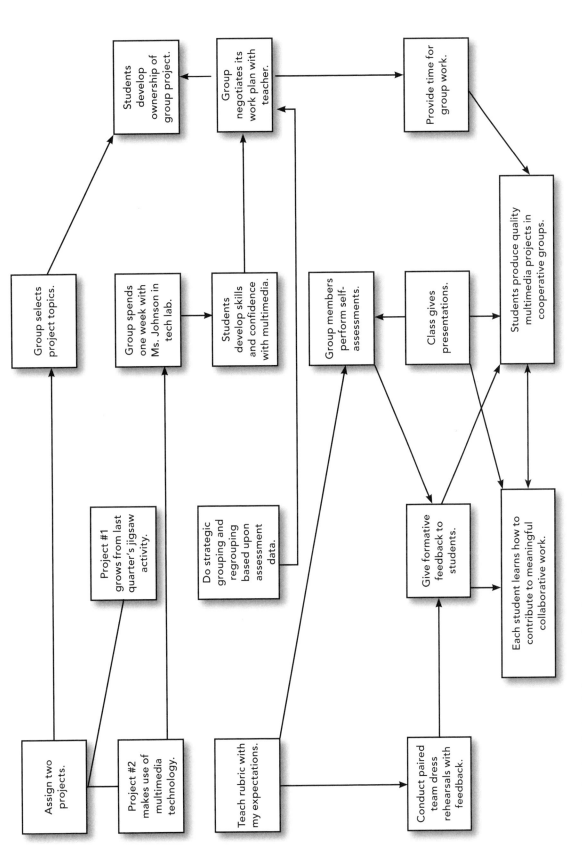

Figure 5.3: Revised visual theory of action after research.

5. **Compare and contrast the alternative revised visual theories of action.** Post the alternative revised theories of action on the wall, and, as a group, discuss the similarities and differences. If your team followed the alternative pilot project model last time, it was because at the beginning of the process, when the PLC team met to generate theories of action, there were divergent perspectives on how to realize universal student success. Things may have changed over the ensuing months. At this point, you are now a more seasoned team. You have conducted pilot projects and have collected data on how students responded to the alternative approaches. Ultimately, nothing alters one's professional perspective more than real classroom data on student performance. Frequently, PLC teams that began with divergent perspectives end up converging on a common plan after having explored the results achieved in alternative pilot projects.

6. **Decide whether to proceed with multiple pilot projects.** As a team, discuss whether your alternative theories of action can or should be reconciled into a single unified theory of action. If the team believes the once divergent perspectives can now be reconciled and chooses to do so, they will be able to say as a PLC team:

    > After having conducted multiple pilot projects, testing alternative theories of action, and reviewing our data, we have concluded that there is one approach that holds with special promise for producing universal student success. Consequently, our entire team will be pursuing this approach next year.

    However, if some team members continue to hold divergent views on the best way to realize universal student success on this achievement target, the team can say:

    > After conducting multiple pilot projects, testing alternative theories of action, and reviewing all the data, we still find promise in multiple approaches for producing universal student success. Consequently, our team decided to conduct another round of alternative pilot projects to enable us to better learn how to meet all of our students' needs.

It is important to recognize that failure to coalesce around a single theory of action is not a defeat. After all, medical doctors continue to use dozens of different antibiotics to treat infections and will frequently employ a variety of treatment regimes for the same illness. Likewise, architects continue to design different structures for clients with similar needs. Until or unless we have evidence that one type of house, office building, or school is superior to all alternatives and in all cases, it is unwise to stifle the creativity of the designers. Clearly the same thing applies for educational architects. Failure to agree on a single set of actions is not necessarily problematic. What is problematic, however, is perpetuating practices that cannot be supported by data.

Sharing the Results: The Nesting Dolls of School Culture

In chapter 1, we used the image of Russian nesting dolls to describe functioning professional learning communities. Specifically, it was said that learning communities exist inside larger learning communities that are themselves part of a broad professional community. Generally, the unit we most identify with in this cultural nest is the PLC team, which consists of those professionals we work most closely with on a daily basis. That being said, in schools that have become transformed into true professional learning communities, individual PLC teams are anything but isolated. It is common for PLC teams in the same school to recognize that they share responsibility for educating the same students and to feel responsible for complementary aspects of the overall school program. In a school wishing to become a true professional learning community, the powerful professional team learning that emanates from locally conducted action research must be accessible to the rest of the faculty.

Schools have used a multitude of vehicles for sharing PLC team action research. Ultimately, schools will need to craft structures and procedures that work for their unique setting. Whatever the dissemination system, it is critical that a school's process for sharing classroom research be supported by the school's leadership, appreciated by the faculty (the membership of the learning community), and adopted as an inseparable part of the fabric of the school. Following are strategies that have been successful for other schools and districts and could easily be incorporated into a custom-designed, action research dissemination model for your professional learning community.

Scheduled Pair-Share Time

Many schools schedule a consistent time for PLC team meetings. Chances are that you and your teammates practiced many of the five habits of inquiry and conducted much of your action research during scheduled PLC team time. Some schools have found it valuable to set aside some scheduled PLC team time (usually once per month or every other month) for cross-group peer sharing. On these days, instead of meeting by themselves for work on their action research, two PLC teams meet together for the sole purpose of sharing and receiving feedback on their work. Teams can share either completed action research projects or works in progress. During these sessions, the two teams take turns sharing their research and soliciting ideas that will help them move their work forward. The process is quite simple: each team presents and explains its visual theory of action (graphic reconstruction) and the shared vision that drove it. They also report any data that have been collected and analyzed. Each team's presentation is followed by questions, answers, and open discussion.

Faculty Meeting Poster Sessions

Schools that follow the poster session process use a regularly scheduled full-faculty meeting to create what is essentially a local education fair. Tables are placed along the perimeter of the room (in large schools, this usually occurs in the gym or cafeteria) where each PLC team displays the work it has underway. It is common at these poster sessions to see colorful trifold posters complete with priority pies, visual theories of action, and displays of data. Throughout the meeting, one or two members of every team remain at their display table to pass out flyers, explain the project, and answer questions. Meanwhile, the other members of the team are free to enjoy refreshments and visit the other displays, where they can learn about the educational architecture their colleagues are creating. Every fifteen minutes, the faculty members manning the booths are relieved, allowing each team member at least a half hour to move about the education fair and learn from the creative work of their colleagues.

The amount of professional learning that can be gained in a relaxed, forty-five-minute review of PLC team–produced displays is extraordinary and exceeds what is normally accomplished in a traditional faculty meeting. Occasionally, a school will schedule their PLC poster session on the afternoon of a school board or PTA meeting. The displays are then left in place for the larger community to observe and enjoy. It is surprising how many parents don't realize that the creation of innovative educational architecture is part of a professional educator's job description. A few minutes wandering through an education fair opens many a parent's eye to the professional world of the classroom teacher.

The Rotating Faculty Meeting

When this strategy is followed, one faculty meeting is hosted each month by a different PLC team (frequently in a different part of the building). Then the principle item on the agenda for the faculty meeting is a sharing of the host team's action research. As with the poster sessions, these presentations can feature recently completed work or work in progress. Teams are free to present their work in many ways. The most common is a handout containing an outline and visuals displaying the shared team vision and theory of action. This is followed by a brief explanation of the methodology (the strategies used for data collection and analysis). If findings have been developed, they are displayed, and time is provided at the end for questions and discussion. A schedule of rotating faculty meetings is a very effective way to institutionalize a schoolwide discourse on action research. It reinforces the reality that participating in collaborative inquiry is a continuous expectation of the school's culture.

A Community Journal

A written or electronic journal is a wonderful way to share the work of PLC teams. I have seen journals that were developed for a single building as well as ones that were used to disseminate information submitted by PLC teams from across a large school district. One virtue of using a journal for dissemination is that it can be read at one's leisure and accessed whenever needed. Journals can also be indexed and archived. This way, as the school or district's professional learning community matures, and as more and more action research is conducted, anyone can access the learning community's rich history of program development and instructional improvement. Occasionally, one will see a district journal looking quite polished and formal, filled with long articles and designed to appear like a traditional professional publication. In other cases, the articles found in a learning community journal are abbreviated, sometimes little more than abstracts. Whatever the format, the journal of a professional learning community should contain, at a minimum, short descriptions of recent studies conducted by local PLC teams and information on how to contact participants for more information.

A School or District Conference

It is not uncommon for schools to schedule an in-service day for the professional development of the faculty. I have visited a number of schools and school districts that use these days as opportunities for members of the professional learning community to learn from each other. This is done by transforming traditional in-service days into high-powered professional educational conferences. At these district action research conferences, all sessions (keynotes and breakout sessions) are presented by local educators or teams of local teachers who share their collaborative action research. The purpose of these in-service day conferences is to acquaint the members of the wider professional learning community about the breadth of the research and development occurring in their midst. Participant evaluations of school district and building action research conferences consistently show that this process for learning from colleagues is rated among the best and most relevant forms of professional development. Ultimately, the powerful message conveyed by holding an annual district educational conference is that the local schools are a rich reservoir of relevant research and development.

Leadership Note

If your school is to become a true professional learning community, it is essential that the learning that can be stimulated through collaborative action research not be limited to the members of the PLC team that carried out a particular project. Leadership must develop, support, and sustain structures that routinize the sharing of locally developed professional knowledge, making the sharing of action research a cultural norm of the school. Among strategies that can help with this are:

- Allow teachers to count PLC team action research efforts toward required supervision and evaluation expectations.

- Use the five-stage action research model for all ad-hoc school improvement work, and make it a requirement that all task forces working on school improvement report back on their research and development to the professional learning community (preferably at faculty meetings).

- Engage in action research on your own leadership and administrative work, and report regularly on your progress. Model your engagement in learning by doing!

- Consider faculty meeting time as a prime resource for professional learning, and exploit that resource in a way that advances the work of the school as a professional learning community.

- Develop a model to institutionalize the sharing and dissemination of the collaborative action research conducted by PLC teams.

Conclusion

Teaching is very hard work, and it is getting more difficult all the time. While most teachers enjoy the very act of spending time with young people, they need and deserve additional rewards for their professional accomplishments. My personal mission in life is to make teaching so rewarding that the best, brightest, most creative, and energetic people in our society find teaching to be an irresistibly attractive career. Collaborative action research has been shown to be a powerful and authentic mechanism for making teaching more rewarding. This is because, above all else, what motivates teachers is helping their students succeed. The credible data that you have now uncovered regarding the effect your educational architecture and professional actions have had on your students are concrete evidence of your professional impact. Teachers who regularly engage in action research, and then use the results of their studies to inform their future teaching, report greater job satisfaction. Finally, nothing makes someone feel better about membership in a professional learning community than the knowledge that her input is valued by peers. Creating cultures where this type of collegial learning is routine practice will result in building schools where the noble profession of teaching will be able to thrive for years to come.

Findings Comparison Chart

Use this chart to write down each finding pertaining to student performance on a particular achievement target in response to Impact Question 2.

Finding	Teacher A	Teacher B	Teacher C	Teacher D

Projected Time Use Form

Based on your action research data, list all the categories of actions that you now feel need to be focused on if every student is to achieve success on this achievement target.

Item: Percentage:

Impact Table

Use this form to track the relationship between instructional action and performance across different classrooms.

Data Source	Instructional Action 1	Instructional Action 2	Instructional Action 3	Instructional Action 4	Instructional Action 5	Instructional Action 6	Instructional Action 7

Action Research Process for PLC Teams

Clarifying a Shared Vision for Success

Strategies:
- Scenario Writing
- Identify Achievement Targets
- Generate Assessment Criteria

Articulating Theories of Action

Strategies:
- Draw Priority Pies
- Create Visual Theories of Action

Acting Purposefully While Collecting Data

Strategies:
- The Three Impact Questions
- Select Data Collection Strategies
- Complete a Data Collection Planning Matrix

Analyzing Data Collaboratively

Strategies:
- Analyze Quantitative Data
- Analyze Qualitative Data
- Conduct a Trend Analysis
- Generate Bulleted Findings
- Conduct Member Checking

Using Informed Team Action Planning

Strategies:
- Compare Findings With Colleagues
- Develop Revised Theories of Action
- Share Results With the Learning Community
- Select Focus for Next Round of Research

Epilogue
Action Research and the Culture of the Professional Learning Community

An organization's culture is often the most important feature distinguishing it from similarly situated organizations. What constitutes a culture are the norms, values, beliefs, and behaviors shared by the members of that community.

Cultures can be categorized in two ways: by their strength and their functionality. There are organizations with tight cultures and others with weak cultures. Likewise, in some organizational cultures the prevailing norms and behaviors are functional, and in others these norms and behaviors are dysfunctional. Functional norms of behavior serve to make an organization more effective in carrying out its goals. Conversely, just as in a dysfunctional family, the prevailing norms and habits of a dysfunctional organization can undermine its stated goals.

By definition, a school that has become a professional learning community is a place with a tight functional culture. If the culture is weak, meaning the norms and habits of behavior are not universally adhered to, it is unlikely that the school can be considered a community by its members. While we may spend our time in a workplace, we only consider ourselves to be part of a community when we feel a deep kinship to the norms and values of the group. Teachers who feel they are part of a true community believe that they share more with their colleagues than proximity. They are bound by a deep commitment to shared norms, values, and behaviors.

Schools where teachers are continually refining their craft, where each day the professionals know more than they did the day before, where the very act of being a member of the community means one is growing, will be schools where students and families are well served. A professional learning community is a functional culture because its members are performing better each day as a result of what they learned the day before and are aware that they are making the world a better place.

Strengthening Your PLC Through the Habits of Inquiry

One nurtures a functional culture by reinforcing those habitual behaviors or norms that are supportive of the community's shared goals. When the shared goal of the community is to foster professional learning for the benefit of students, then it is important to identify and nurture the specific norms and habits that can contribute to professional learning. It should come as no surprise that I see the five habits of inquiry that have framed this book as critical for nurturing and strengthening the culture of any professional learning community, as follows.

Habit of Inquiry 1: Clarifying a Shared Vision for Success

The essence of this habit of inquiry is regular discussion of valued outcomes. In schools where the normal discourse is framed around what people are reaching for—shared community goals and shared dreams for student success—people will be less likely to accept anything less than universally high achievement. We reinforce this habit of inquiry whenever we set goals for our programs. However, we are also practicing this habit when, in casual conversation, we find ourselves asking a colleague, "What are you working on? Tell me what you are trying to accomplish."

Habit of Inquiry 2: Articulating Theories of Action

Two hallmarks of a professional learning community are the twin beliefs that (1) there is always more to be learned and (2) learning by doing is exciting. When you were developing and elaborating your theory of action to guide your action research, you were demonstrating your curiosity and willingness to experiment with new ideas. But building formal theories of action isn't the only way we demonstrate our inventiveness. You reinforce this same habit of inquiry whenever you are overheard pondering, "I wonder if . . . ?" or whenever you find yourself inquiring of a colleague, "How are you doing that?" or "Why are you doing it that way?"

Habit of Inquiry 3: Acting Purposefully While Collecting Data

In professional learning communities, it is the norm to regularly monitor the results of one's professional actions. The very act of collecting data on one's actions is an act of faith in the learning process. When students and colleagues see us asking questions and collecting data, they realize we want to know how things are working and that, if things aren't proceeding as we'd like, we possess the wherewithal to create change. This habit of inquiry will have become part of your school's culture when you expect to be asked and enjoy answering the question, "Why are you doing that?"

Habit of Inquiry 4: Analyzing Data Collaboratively

For purposes of professional learning one of the best features about teacher-conducted collaborative action research is that the insights we acquire can be put to good use immediately.

When analyzing your action research data, you went through a deliberate process designed to uncover the story embedded in the data you collected. Drawing conclusions from action research data is a valuable exercise of this habit of inquiry, but it is not the only time you get to practice this habit. When the spirit of data analysis has been internalized and has become habitual in a school, an atmosphere of curiosity inevitably emerges. You will know when that habit has taken hold in your school by listening to the professional discourse. The spirit of analysis is part of a school's culture if, whenever something unusual occurs in class or happens at the school, everyone's first instinct is to ask, "Why?" Whenever we are asking our colleagues to join us in exploring the rationale behind a proposal, we are reinforcing the powerful norm of data analysis.

Habit of Inquiry 5: Using Informed Team Action Planning

It has been said that teaching is the world's second most private act. This is not the case in professional learning communities. By definition, these are schools where teaching has become deprivatized and responsibility for student learning is a shared value. When you designed your revised theory of action with your PLC team, you were engaged in informed team action planning. Furthermore, the plans that emerged from your action research were the result of hours of thoughtful collaborative work. One powerful insight into whether this habit has taken hold in your school or within your team is how often you hear colleagues discussing instructional programs with the use of the plural possessive *our* as opposed to the singular *my*. The more it becomes routine to think of school programs as something we all share, the more ingrained this habit has become.

A strong culture has its central values reinforced through both big events and daily routines, through individual interactions and group activities, by the things it celebrates with great fanfare and the things that simply bring a smile to someone's face. This dynamic relationship between the individual and community is what makes a professional learning community truly vibrant.

* * * * *

Hopefully, the ideas in this book helped you discover new realms of creativity in your teaching. If this happened, I hope it resulted in your feeling good about yourself and your chosen profession. I am confident that if you take the time to share what you learned, it will make others in your professional learning community happy that they have you as a colleague. It is my hope that by exercising the five habits of inquiry and engaging in the creative work of designing a new generation of educational architecture, you will find more personal satisfaction in your professional work, and that we will all move ever closer to realizing universal student success.

Appendix
Ethics and Collaborative Action Research

Two areas of ethical consideration have relevance to the collaborative action research you may conduct in your role as a professional educator. The first pertains to professional ethics and the second to research ethics.

Professional Ethics

As a professional, you have a sacred obligation to your clients. Every time you enter the classroom, you are obligated to deliver instruction in the best manner you know how. When you deliver on this obligation, you show yourself to be an ethical professional educator. Fundamentally, the only reason to engage in action research, as promoted in this book, is to provide students with the best possible instruction. For this reason, conducting action research is no more than an expression of your devotion to the ethics of your profession.

Research Ethics

In the United States, as well as most other countries, there are laws and procedures that must be adhered to whenever one conducts research involving human subjects. The purpose of these procedures is to ensure that no one is ever unknowingly subjected to experimental manipulation or placed at risk for the purposes of scientific research without prior knowledge and permission. The law specifically exempts the following:

> Research conducted in established or commonly accepted educational settings, involving normal educational practices, such as (1) research on regular and special education instructional strategies, or (2) research on the effectiveness of or the comparison among instructional techniques, curricula, or classroom management methods. (National Institutes of Health, 2005)

Most action research, as conducted by practicing educators, fits under this exemption. The primary reason that teacher action research isn't considered regulated research has to do with the rationale for engaging in the inquiry and collecting the data—namely, the improvement of instruction. Most people would agree that a teacher who didn't collect and use data on students' learning when planning instruction wasn't doing his or her job in a professional manner. Similarly, when a doctor orders tests and considers the results when planning the patient's treatment, it is simply considered good practice, not medical research. What is critical from a professional and ethics standpoint is that the student (or patient) knows the service provider is making decisions solely on the basis of a professional commitment to providing the best care possible.

Occasionally, research is conducted in schools to generate knowledge, not instructional improvement—for example, when graduate students doing doctoral research collect data at a school. Prior to commencing that type of research, formal approval needs to be obtained from the institutional review boards (IRB) of the sponsoring university and school district. Federal regulations require that an agency's IRB review and approve all human subject research proposals to ensure that the rights of human subjects are protected.

The action research discussed in this book is not considered regulated human subject research for the following reasons:

1. All data collected are for educational purposes.

2. Students will receive the same treatment (instruction) they would have received, whether or not their teacher had conducted action research.

3. Ultimately, the subjects in our action research studies aren't the students. To the degree that there may be a human subject, it is us (the teachers), and our instruction that are the objects of scrutiny.

For all of these reasons, you can consider conducting action research and the sharing of your learning with your building colleagues to be within the confines of good professional practice, governed simply by your professional obligation to provide the best possible education you can provide. That being said, there are several reasons why you may wish to consider going the extra mile and acquiring student or parental permission prior to collecting action research data.

Informed Consent

Before you can make use of a human being as a subject in scientific research, you must request and receive prior written consent from each subject. If that subject is a minor, you must obtain the permission from the minor's parent or guardian. As a rule, the subject is consenting to two things: first, to being subjected to the experimental condition, and second, to having his or her words, ideas, or visage used in reports of the research. Since the only interventions your students will be exposed to involve your instruction (which they would be experiencing anyway), there is no experimental intervention for the student or parent to consent to. Furthermore, the sharing of student information among school faculty is permissible and protected professional behavior. The only reason why, as an action researcher, you might feel a need for prior informed consent is if, at some point, you wished to disseminate your research more widely and in doing so would be unable to mask the identities of everyone involved.

Parental Permission

Many teachers go the extra step of formally obtaining prior student and parental permission for the use of student work, opinions, and data in their studies. Personally, I like this idea since I find that this extra step can serve several valuable purposes: it enhances home–school communication, increases trust, and is good public relations. I use the permission letters to inform my students and parents of my professional commitment to glean as much learning as possible from my teaching. In my experience, letting my students know how serious I am about my teaching tends to result in their taking it more seriously as well. As a final benefit, by routinely securing permission before doing my research, I avoid having to do so after the fact, should later I decide I want to write or make a presentation about it. In the very rare case when a student or parent denied me permission, I simply omitted that student from my sample. For example, in a report of my research, I would say,

> This study was conducted in an eighth-grade language arts class. The class had thirty-two students enrolled; however, permission was only obtained to collect and report data on thirty students. Consequently, this study reports on the data obtained from thirty of thirty-two students.

You may wish to adapt this sample permission letter for use with your action research.

> Dear Parent,
>
> This year I am working with several teachers in an effort to improve _____. When teachers systematically examine their teaching in this way, it is called *action research*. Our goal through action research is to learn as much as we can about our teaching, so we can improve our techniques to ensure that every student will be successful in our classes.
>
> As part of my action research, I would like to review and analyze the work done by each of my students. Additionally, I would like to ask the students for their feedback on my instruction.
>
> I am writing to ask for your permission to use your student's work and opinions with my action research. I am requesting this because your student's work and opinions will help me become a better teacher. If permission is granted, and should I ever make a report on this research, I will do everything possible to maintain confidentiality and ensure that your child cannot be identified.
>
> Finally, I promise that your child will receive the same instruction, benefits, and commitment from me whether you grant your permission or not.
>
> If I have your permission to use [student's name] work and ideas in my action research, please return this form with your approval.
>
> Sincerely,
>
> [Teacher's name]
>
> I grant permission for the use of [child's full name] ideas, schoolwork, and words in the action research conducted this year by his or her teacher, [teacher's name].

I understand that if permission isn't granted, my student will not be denied any educational opportunities. I understand that everything possible will be done to maintain confidentiality in any reports of this research.

Parent Signature: _____

Date: _____

Other Ethical Considerations

Beyond obtaining parental permission, it is suggested that you follow these guidelines:

1. Never audiotape or videotape anyone surreptitiously.

2. Use pseudonyms or student numbers in place of actual student names in any written reports of your research.

3. Report on your research to your students and parents. Give them a firsthand account of what you've learned and what you are learning.

* * * * *

The decision to invest your energy in the conduct of action research is an expression of dedication to your professionalism. Not only will your research provide you with valuable information that will enable you to better meet your students' needs, but it will provide your colleagues with data to foster school improvement. Taking a little time prior to conducting your inquiry to consider these issues of professional and research ethics should ensure that parents and students will understand and appreciate your efforts.

References

Allington, R. L. (2002). *Big brother and the national reading curriculum: How ideology trumped evidence.* Portsmouth, NH: Heinemann.

Conzemius, A., & O'Neill, J. (2002). *The handbook for SMART school teams.* Bloomington, IN: Solution Tree Press.

Creswell, J. W. (2009). *Research design: Qualitative, quantitative, and mixed methods approaches* (3rd ed.). Thousand Oaks, CA: Sage.

DuFour, R., DuFour, R., & Eaker, R. (2008). *Revisiting professional learning communities at work: New insights for improving schools.* Bloomington, IN: Solution Tree Press.

Garmston, R. (2005). Group wise: No time for learning? Just take it in tin bites and savor it. *Journal of Staff Development, 26*(4), 65.

Glickman, C. D. (1993). *Renewing America's schools: A guide for school-based action.* San Francisco: Jossey-Bass.

Glickman, C. D. (2002). *Leadership for learning: How to help teachers succeed.* Alexandria, VA: Association for Supervision and Curriculum Development.

Guskey, T. R. (2001). The backward approach. *Journal of Staff Development, 22*(3), 60.

Heifetz, R. A., & Linsky, M. (2002). *Leadership on the line: Staying alive through the dangers of leading.* Boston: Harvard Business School.

Hord, S. (1997). *Professional learning communities: Communities of continuous inquiry and improvement.* Austin, TX: Southwest Educational Development Laboratory.

Lewin, K., & Cartwright, D. (Ed.). (1951). *Field theory in social science: Selected theoretical papers.* New York: Harper & Row.

Los Angeles Unified School District. (n.d.) *Fidelity of implementation.* Accessed at www.lausd.k12.ca.us/lausd/offices/hep/news/fidelity.html on April 2, 2010.

Martin, K. A., Moritz, S. E., & Hall, C. R. (1999). Imagery use in sport: A literature review and applied model. *Sport Psychologist, 13*(3), 245–268.

McIntyre, E., Powell, R., Coots, K. B., Jones, D., Powers, S., Deeters, F., & Petrosko, J. (2005). Reading instruction in the NCLB era: Teachers' implementation fidelity of early reading models. *Educational Research & Policy Studies, 5*(2), 66–102.

Miles, M. B., & Huberman, A. M. (1994). *Qualitative data analysis: An expanded sourcebook* (2nd ed.). Thousand Oaks, CA: Sage.

National Institutes of Health. (2005). *Regulations and ethical guidelines* (Title 45, Part 46). Accessed at http://ohsr.od.nih.gov/guidelines/45cfr46.html on May 16, 2009.

Sagor, R. (1981). A day in the life: A technique for assessing school climate and effectiveness. *Educational Leadership, 39*(3), 190–193.

Sagor, R. (1992a). *How to conduct collaborative action research*. Alexandria, VA: Association for Supervision and Curriculum Development.

Sagor, R. (1992b). *Collaborative action research: A cultural mechanism for school development and professional restructuring?* Paper presented at the annual meeting of the American Educational Research Association, San Francisco, CA.

Sagor, R. (1995). Overcoming the one-solution syndrome. *Educational Leadership, 52*(7), 24–27.

Sagor, R. (2000). *Guiding school improvement with action research*. Alexandria, VA: Association for Supervision and Curriculum Development.

Sagor, R. (2003). *Motivating students and teachers in an era of standards*. Alexandria, VA: Association for Supervision and Curriculum Development.

Sagor, R. (2005). *The action research guidebook: A four-step process for educators and school teams*. Thousand Oaks, CA: Corwin.

Smith, K. J. (2006). A successful day? Engaging your students may not be enough. In K. J. Smith, *The First Year* (pp. 25–26). Chapel Hill, NC: LEARN North Carolina. Accessed at www.learnnc.org/lp/pages/259 on May 12, 2009.

Stiggins, R. J. (2001). *Student-involved classroom assessment* (3rd ed.). Upper Saddle River, NJ: Merrill Prentice Hall.

Tashakkori, A., & Teddlie, C. (Eds.). (2003). *Handbook of mixed methods in social and behavioral research*. Thousand Oaks, CA: Sage.

Townsend, T. (Ed.). (2007). *International handbook of school effectiveness and improvement*. Dordrecht, the Netherlands: Springer.

U.S. Department of Transportation, National Highway Traffic Safety Administration. (2001). *Process and outcome evaluation of the Buckle Up America initiatives* (DOT HS 809 272). Washington, DC: Author. Accessed at www.nhtsa.dot.gov/people/injury/research/buckle up/ii__trends.htm on April 2, 2010.

Wallace, F., Blasé, K., Fixsen, D., & Naoom, S. (2008). *Implementing the findings of research: Bridging the gap between knowledge and practice.* Alexandria, VA: Educational Research Service.

WestEd. (2000). *Teachers who learn, kids who achieve: A look at schools with model professional development.* San Francisco: Author. (ERIC Document Reproduction Service No. ED440102)

Wiggins, G., & McTighe, J. (1998). *Understanding by design.* Alexandria, VA: Association for Supervision and Curriculum Development.

Index

Raising the Bar and Closing the Gap
Whatever It Takes
Richard DuFour, Rebecca DuFour, Robert Eaker, and Gayle Karhanek
This sequel to the best-selling *Whatever It Takes: How Professional Learning Communities Respond When Kids Don't Learn* expands on original ideas and presses further with new insights. Foundational concepts combine with real-life examples of schools throughout North America that have gone from traditional cultures to PLCs. **BKF378**

Differentiated Professional Development in a Professional Learning Community
Linda Bowgren and Kathryn Sever
If differentiated instruction works for students, why not apply it to teacher learning? A practical guide for designing school or district professional development plans, this book explains a three-step model that is core to the differentiation process. **BKF275**

Learning by Doing
A Handbook for Professional Learning Communities at Work™
Richard DuFour, Rebecca DuFour, Robert Eaker, and Thomas Many
The second edition of *Learning by Doing* is an action guide for closing the knowing-doing gap and transforming schools into PLCs. It also includes seven major additions that equip educators with essential tools for confronting challenges. **BKF416**

The Power of Professional Learning Communities at Work™:
Bringing the Big Ideas to Life
Featuring Richard DuFour, Robert Eaker, and Rebecca DuFour
This four-program video series takes you inside eight diverse schools, where teachers and administrators engage in candid conversations and collaborative team meetings. See how successful schools radically improve student learning, and learn the fundamentals of PLC with this powerful, fun staff development tool. **VIF094**

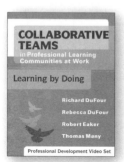

Collaborative Teams in Professional Learning Communities at Work™
Learning by Doing
By Richard DuFour, Rebecca DuFour, Robert Eaker, and Thomas Many
This video shows exactly what collaborative teams do. Aligned with the best-selling book *Learning by Doing*, it features unscripted footage of collaboration in action. Learn how teams organize, interact, and find time to meet; what products they produce; and more. **DVF023**

Solution Tree | Press   *a division of*   Solution Tree   Visit solution-tree.com or call 800.733.6786 to order.